God, Jesus, and the Ancestors

Marco Lazzarotti

God, Jesus, and the Ancestors

An Ethnography of the Ancestors' Rites in the Taiwanese Catholic Church

Marco Lazzarotti  https://orcid.org/0000-0003-3313-8674

Bibliographic information published by the Deutsche Nationalbibliothek
The Deutsche Nationalbibliothek lists this publication in the Deutsche Nationalbibliografie; detailed bibliographic data are available in the Internet at http://dnb.dnb.de.

This book is published under the Creative Commons Attribution License CC BY-SA 4.0. The cover is subject to the Creative Commons License CC BY-ND 4.0.

Published by Heidelberg Asian Studies Publishing (HASP), 2023

Heidelberg University / Heidelberg University Library
Heidelberg Asian Studies Publishing (HASP),
Grabengasse 1, 69117 Heidelberg, Germany
https://hasp.ub.uni-heidelberg.de

The electronic open–access version of this work is permanently available on the website of Heidelberg Asian Studies Publishing:
https://hasp.ub.uni-heidelberg.de
urn: urn:nbn:de:bsz:16-hasp-1210-0
doi: https://doi.org/10.11588/hasp.1210

Text © 2023, Marco Lazzarotti

Cover illustration: Cover image © 2023 Ching–Ho Chen

ISBN 978-3-948791-65-0 (Softcover)
ISBN 978-3-948791-64-3 (PDF)

Contents

List of Figures   vii

Acknowledgments   ix

List of Abbreviations   xi

Notes on Romanization and Chinese Characters   xiii

1 Introduction   1
- 1.1 On Occidentalism 1
- 1.2 Otherness and Daily Life 2
- 1.3 On Ancestors 3
- 1.4 Contact of Cultures 5
  - 1.4.1 Historical Contacts 8
- 1.5 *Jian* 間: Where History and Culture meet 9
- 1.6 God, Jesus, and the Ancestors 11

2 Anthropologists and Ancestors   15
- 2.1 A Brief Literature Review 15
- 2.2 The Ancestors' Rites and the other imported Religions 21
- 2.3 A Case of Cultural Encounter 24
- 2.4 Person as a *jian* 間: The Space where Cultures Meet 31

3 Catholicism in Taiwan, History and Anthropology   33
- 3.1 The Chinese Rites Controversy 33
  - 3.1.1 Anthropological Considerations of the Chinese Rites Controversy 39
- 3.2 Catholicism in Taiwan 41
  - 3.2.1 The First Evangelization (1626-1642) 42
  - 3.2.2 The Second Evangelization (1859-1895) 44
  - 3.2.3 The Third Period (1895-1945) 46
  - 3.2.4 The Fourth Period 47
- 3.3 Some Anthropological Considerations 50

4 Fieldwork   55
- 4.1 Fieldwork Place 55
  - 4.1.1 Who are the Faithful? 58
  - 4.1.2 Experiences of Conversion 60
- 4.2 The Taiwanese Catholic Ancestors' Rites 63

5 Cultural Interpretations   69
- 5.1 The same service to the dead as to the living 事死如事生 . . 70
- 5.2 The Concept of Time 72
  - 5.2.1 Lunar Calendar 72
  - 5.2.2 Gregorian Solar Calendar and Liturgical Time 73
- 5.3 The Concept of *Ling* 靈 76
  - 5.3.1 Chinese *Ling* and Christian Miracles 78

6 Gods, Ghosts, and the Ancestors   81
- 6.1 Gods 81
  - 6.1.1 The Blessed Virgin Mary 82
- 6.2 Ancestors 84
  - 6.2.1 Ancestors and the Catholic Church 96
  - 6.2.2 Funerals 99
- 6.3 Ghosts 108

7 Conclusions   115
- 7.1 A Dialogue of Cultures 115
- 7.2 The Place of the Dialogue 117
- 7.3 The Textile of Dialogue 119

Bibliography   121

List of Figures

1	Location of the Resurrection Church	58
2	Ancestors' Ceremonies in the Resurrection Church	64
3	The Blessed Virgin Mary (a) and Guanyin (b), painted in traditional Chinese dress and holding a baby	83
4	Ancestor Tablets in the Jilin Road Church, Taipei	86
5	The Altar (a) and the Ancestors' Tablet (b) of Mr. Li, Taipei	89
6	Detail of the altar of the ancestors of Mr. Li (a) and Mr. Zhang (b), Taipei	91
7	Detail of the ancestor tablets of Mr. Li (a) and Mr. Zhang (b), Taipei	93
8	Outline of the tablet for the Parish (a) and for the deceased parishioner (b)	94
9	fuhuozhi 復活紙	98
10	Resurrection Papers on a Traditional Tomb, Taichung	98
11	The division of seats inside the church during the funeral. 中國主教團禮儀委員會Bishop Conference of China, 殯葬禮儀 (Taipei: Xiuding, 1989)	101
12	The Taoist paper house inside the Church of the Resurrection, Taipei	106

Acknowledgments

I am sure that some of the more experienced readers have already noticed the parallel between the title of my book and the article by Arthur Wolf, "Gods, Ghosts and Ancestors," which Wolf wrote in 1974[1]. That article was my first approach to the study of Taiwanese Popular Religion and ancestor worship. I hope the title could be a way to direct my research into the research field that he helped to open and develop. Before starting to introduce the result of my research, I hope the reader will allow me to say a few words to thank all the people behind the making of this book. Firstly, all the faithful of the Resurrection church. They not only welcomed and accepted me as a brother but also with endless patience answered my questions and collaborated with me during my fieldwork.

I am forever indebted to my supervisor, professor 葉春榮 Chuen–rong Yeh, who introduced me to this area of debate and relentlessly guided me through the process of elaborating the material I collected. He helped me, especially during the writing of my M.A. thesis from which this book comes.

I would like to thank all my missionary friends who helped, encouraged, and gave me support during the time of my research (and not only during my research), particularly Fr. Edi, Fr. Fabrizio, Fr. Giuseppe, and Fr. Paulin with was working on a topic very similar to mine. I would like to thank them, especially for all the discussions we had together. With their suggestions and their corrections, they made me feel how much they cared about me, and also about my research.

Other significant thanks must be addressed to the professors and classmates of the Taiwan National University for their constant support and encouragement. A special mention to professor 童 Tong and the dear departed professor 嚴 Yan for their invaluable advice and to my classmates Yi ling 宜羚, Yi zhi 伊知, Ying ru 應如, Nai wen 乃雯, Yu sheng 育生, Ai lun 艾倫, Zong zheng 宗正, Ling Yin 苓尹, Fang ru 凡如, xiao Bai 小白, the teacher assistants, Jing wen 靜文e Yu ding 鈺釘, Mr. Chen 陳, Mr. Du 杜, and xiao Wang 小王. Their friendship is the most beautiful among my Taiwanese experiences. I cannot forget to thank Martin, Jackie, Paul, Linda, and Frank John for their efforts in trying to fix my "Italian–English."

---

1. Arthur P. Wolf, "Gods, ghosts, and ancestors," in *Religion and ritual in Chinese society* (Stanford: California : Univ. Pr, 1974), 131–182.

Acknowledgments

And last (but not least) I would like to thank my wife Joo Young. During the writing of my thesis, she kept a constant smile on her face and bore all my complaints, new theories, and monologues.

Thanks to all of these people and also to those who, because of my ingratitude, I forgot to mention on these pages. May my gratitude be with them, wherever they are.

All sorts of mistakes or inaccuracies in this text are entirely my own responsibility.

List of Abbreviations

CCP	Chinese Communist Party (Zhongguo gongchandang 中國共產黨)
KMT	Kuomintang (Guomindang 國民黨)
PRC	People's Republic of China (Zhonghua Renmin Gongheguo 中華人民共和國)
ROC	Republic of China (Zhonghua Minguo 中華民國)
USA	United States of America

Notes on Romanization and Chinese Characters

This thesis uses Hanyu Pinyin 漢語拼音 romanization. Given names are capitalized. Pinyin words are set in italics unless they represent a given name or a name of an institution. In the transcription of institutions, only the first word is capitalized. Compound words are written together. Pinyin article titles are not italicized. Taiwanese Hokkien is transcribed using the Taiwanese Romanization System (Tâi-uân Bân-lâm-gí Lô-má-jī Phing-im Hong-àn 臺灣閩南語羅馬字拼音方案).

Chapter 1

Introduction

1.1 On Occidentalism

When I started my M.A. at the National Taiwan University, it was very common, at least in the Department of Anthropology, to hear sentences like "because the author of this book is a Western anthropologist, thus he cannot fully understand the effective essence of Chinese culture." A few semesters later, when I attended the class "Religion of Han People" I studied a lot of Western anthropologists who, in the words of my classmate, "were not able to catch the real essence of the Han people's religion." Helped by this kind of environment, I discovered for the first time in my life that Western people are indisputably Orientalists. And that I was undoubtedly one of them. This new enlightened condition (a Westerner who discovers that he is a Westerner) opened my eyes and caused me several problems. When I started to collect data for my fieldwork, one of the problems that I met concerned the meaning of the term "ritual" (*Yishi*, 儀式). I am persuaded that in Western views, terms such as ritual, rite, or ceremonies, are in some ways connected with Turner's concept of *liminalitas*. The ritual is a process where the passage from individuals to collective and from collective to individuals are the crucial moments of the performance. This kind of process involves both temporal and social spheres of experience[1].

The idea of rites is thus linked with the concept of process, but – and this was my trouble – how could the Taiwanese people's concept of rites be defined? The *Pudu* ceremonies (普渡) are certainly rites, but what of the practices performed every morning in front of the ancestors' shrines? Are these considered by Taiwanese people as rites? Is it possible to define them as acts of worship? Similarly, every day quite a number of people put incense sticks outside of their main door, or in the kitchen, or burn paper

---

[1]. Victor Turner, *The Ritual Process: Structure and Anti-Structure* (Transaction Publishers, 1995).

1 Introduction

money at least twice a month. Are these rituals? Are these felt as rites by Taiwanese people? Using my Western way of thinking and according to my own personal feeling, I would surely define them as rituals. But after my fieldwork, and – more importantly – after more than five years of living in Taipei, I started to remodel many of my definitions.

It all started when, during my fieldwork and full of ethnographic zeal, I prepared several clear, direct, and exhaustive questions for my Catholic informers. The first question was roughly formulated in this way: "Do you perform any rites in front of your ancestors' shrine?" And the answer was invariable: "no, I don't perform any particular rite." But when I asked if they used incense sticks to pray for their ancestors the answer was: "yes, every morning I burn incense sticks in front of my ancestor's shrine and I pray for them the rosary or other prayers." Exactly the answer that I was waiting for to the first question!

Conscious that I am going to increase the number of pitiful anthropologists who studied the world of Han people without getting to the bottom of it, I nonetheless did my research in order to better understand the cultural contact between the Catholic religion (*tianzhujiao* 天主教) and the Taiwanese popular religion (*minjianzongjiao* 民間宗教). In order to fulfill this topic, I used as a case study the ancestors' rites that symbolize one of the richest points of discussion between these two different cultural systems.

1.2 Otherness and Daily Life

There are several reasons that convinced me to address this topic. One of them could be summarized by the feeling of difference that I felt when I took part in a Sunday Mass in Taiwan for the first time. I was impressed by several rituals taking place during the liturgy, for instance, the burning of little sticks of incense as I saw doing in many temples (the mass was performed during the Chinese New Year), or by the bow made in front of the ancestors' tables at the end of the Mass, or finally – might not be so shocking but still full of meaning – by the sharing the sign of peace, a unique rite inside the Mass liturgy. As is my custom, I reached out my hand to the man who sat next to me, but he bowed at me with a smiling face, leaving me astonished with my hand hanging in the air. These experiences stimulated several reflections upon the process of acculturation that the Catholic Church is still synthesizing in the Taiwanese contest.

Catholics in Taiwan live in a completely non-Catholic environment. Often only one member of the family is Catholic, while the rest still believe in practices of the Taiwan Popular religion[2]. Most of the time, during the Chinese New Year (*chunjie* 春節) or during Tomb Sweeping Day (*qingmingjie* 清明節), Catholics join their parents and families in praying for their ances-

---

2. In my work, following the indication of Professor Philip Clart (2006), I will use the term Popular Religion instead of the term Folk Religion.

tors, and sometimes they go with them to the temple to burn incense and offer and food to the gods.

This topic gave me the opportunity to confront myself and my studies with people (the Taiwanese Catholics) who daily and naturally live inside two cultural systems; they are a type of bridge, a kind of free land where the encounter of two different symbolic systems takes shape. In the space created by this encounter, the ancestors' rites are the more evident symbol shared by these two cultures. In a certain sense, it is possible to say that I chose this topic, the ancestors' rites as performed inside the Catholic Church, not because of its particularity, but because of its normality. It is plain to all who work in the ethnological field that "Primitive Societies," as described by the works of last-century anthropologists, no longer exist. Nobody, and more importantly, no social group is an island. People and society are interconnected to each other. The emigration/immigration phenomena and the experience of globalization let people meet – and sometimes collide – in their daily life, with different cultures, with a sense of otherness, with "mestizo" (I am Italian, my wife is Korean, we live in Germany and we use Chinese to communicate). Otherness is, without doubt, our daily bread.

The particular situation of the Taiwanese Catholics gave me the opportunity to collect the experiences of people who naturally live inside two different – and in some cases conflicting – cultural systems. These cultural systems are created by centuries of history and have cohabited since the time of the arrival of Christianity in China. This encounter took on a different shape depending on the always-changing historical context in which it develops. Changes in the historical context bring changes in the characteristics which form this encounter. Within the framework of this encounter, the cult of ancestors occupied and still occupies one of the most important places.

1.3 On Ancestors

Ancestors are considered one of the most important points in Han (漢) culture. Traditionally, every family, every Chinese person must pray for his ancestors. This concept permeates the complex and deep Han culture, and it is very present in the everyday life of most Han people. In these pages, I will describe how Taiwanese Catholics honor their ancestors and how the rites that Taiwanese Catholic faithful perform at home or in the church, represent a link between the two cultural systems, the Han popular religion and the Catholic one. In many Taiwanese Catholic homes, it is quite common to find ancestors' altars in the living room, or at least, pictures representing familiar ancestors. During Chinese New Year, some Taiwanese Catholics burn incense and offer food and wine in front of their ancestor's tablets. Inside the churches, special ceremonies are performed in honor and

1 Introduction

remembrance of the ancestors. These performances are considered to be the proper way of commemorating and honoring the dead.

Taiwanese Catholics, especially if newly converted, often wonder whether ancestors' veneration is compatible with the Catholic faith. It is a question with a history that has very deep roots, which dates back four centuries ago, to the beginnings of the time of Matteo Ricci (*Limadou* 利瑪竇)[3].

In the course of history, these practices became the most controversial point inside the Chinese Catholic Church, raising a debate that protracted itself for centuries (See Chapter 3). Even today, although these rituals have been allowed by the ecclesiastical authorities, the dispute, in different ways, still continues. The cultural reverence for ancestors had a significant influence not only within the Catholic Church. Similarly, even though nowadays these practices are banned by most Protestant churches, these practices raised a long discussion inside the Christian Protestant Church[4]. Looking outside the Christian context, these practices and their cultural implications deeply influenced the religious symbols of the Buddhist tradition[5].

Limiting the field to ethnographic research only, it is possible to see how the topic of ancestors has been widely discussed. Since Freedman[6] and Francis Hsu[7] anthropologists have continued to research and study the worship of ancestors among Han people. These studies have already described the phenomenon of ancestors' worship, and its relation with geomantic omens, lineage, kinship, family division, and so on. In Taiwan, research on this topic was performed by many distinguished anthropologists. I will only cite Ahern[8], Wolf[9], Feuchwang[10], Harrel[11], Li Yih–Yuan[12], Wang Song–hsing[13]. I have tried to examine this particular phenomenon – the encounter and co-

---

3. Matteo Ricci (1552–1610) was an Italian Jesuit priest and one of the founding figures of the Jesuit mission in China

4. James Thayer Addison, "Chinese Ancestor-Worship and Protestant Christianity," *The Journal of Religion* 5, no. 2 (1925): 140–149.

5. Stephen F. Teiser, *The Ghost Festival in Medieval China* (Princeton University Press, 1988); Chun-Fang Yu, *Kuan-yin: The Chinese Transformation of Avalokiteśvara* (Columbia University Press, 2001); Batairwa, "What Do You Do When Visiting a Temple," *Quaderni del Centro Studi Asiatico* 1, no. 1 (2006): 70–76.

6. Maurice Freedman, *Lineage organization in Southeastern China*, Monographs on social anthropology / London School of Economics, no. 18 (London: Athlone Press, 1958).

7. Francis Hsu, *Under the Ancestors' Shadow: Kinship, Personality, and Social Mobility in Village China* (Stanford University Press, 1967).

8. Emily M. Ahern, *The Cult of the Dead in a Chinese Village* (Stanford University Press, 1973).

9. Wolf, "Gods, ghosts, and ancestors."

10. Stephan Feuchtwang, "Domestic and communal worship in Taiwan," in *Religion and ritual in Chinese society*, Arthur P. Wolf (Editor) (Stanford University Press., 1974), 105–129.

11. Stevan Harrell, "The ancestors at home: domestic worship in a land-poor Taiwanese village," in *Ancestors*, edited by William H. Newell (The Hague, 1976), 373–385.

12. Yih-yuan Li, "Chinese geomancy and ancestor worship: a further discussion," in *Ancestors*, edited by William H. Newell (De Gruyter Mouton, 1976), 329–338.

13. Sung-hsing Wang, "Ancestors proper and peripheral," in *Ancestors*, edited by William H. Newell (De Gruyter Mouton, 1976), 365–372.

habitation of two religions in Taiwan – as an encounter not only between two religions or between two cosmologies, but as an encounter between two cultures, between two complexes, and, in some ways antithetic cultural systems. It is my deep conviction that it is possible to approach and analyze the phenomenon of the ancestors' rites as performed by the Taiwanese Catholics, only by placing it within a larger contextual framework of history and culture. It is thus necessary to put the situation of the Catholic Church in Taiwan into a framework defined by the above-mentioned concepts: as a new symbolic system that merges into a preexisting one. To the old symbolic system are added – through the development of history – new symbols, which are translated and interpreted according to the cultural frames by which people orient and give meaning to their actions. This happens because, as stated by Geertz, symbols "are historically constructed, socially maintained, and individually applied"[14]. Each person, thus, uses the symbols that in a particular moment and situation will help her/him to solve the problems that emerge in everyday life.

From this point of view, it is possible to understand why, within the phenomenon of conversion, different tendencies are present: there are people who embrace the new faith and people who oppose it, among the faithful, there are very observant believers who attend constantly to the rites of the Church, while some others don't go to the Church and still participate in activities of the Taiwanese popular religion, such as temple festivals, and so on. This approach to understanding would be helpful because, among the Catholics, there are people who choose to keep their ancestors' related rituals, and people who decide to give up their ancestors' tablets.

1.4 Contact of Cultures

Geertz defines religion as a cultural system, "a system of symbols which acts to establish powerful, pervasive, and long-lasting moods and motivations in men by formulating conceptions of a general order of existence and clothing these conceptions with such an aura of factuality that the moods and motivations seem uniquely realistic"[15]. In his definition of religion, Geertz stressed the importance of religious symbols which according to him play a very important role in the everyday life of people, giving to everyone terms of judgment for the interpretation of life experiences, and for assigning moral, intellectual, and emotional value to these experiences. I totally agree with the extreme importance that Geertz assigned to the religious symbols, these symbols are powerful for they not only invoke deep moral sentiments concerning how the world should be but they also shape human

---

14. Clifford Geertz, "Time, Person and Conduct in Bali," in *The interpretation of cultures: selected essays* (New York: Basic Books, 1973), 364.

15. Clifford Geertz, "Religion as a Cultural System," in *The interpretation of cultures: selected essays* (New York: Basic Books, 1973), 90.

1 Introduction

behavior and influence how human beings interpret reality. They provide a representation of the way things are and guide human activity. Religious symbol systems also formulate conceptions of general order in which they form a part of the worldview that shares unquestioned assumptions about the world and how it works. When co-religionists and devotees act together, they begin to accept the group's symbolic interpretations of the world as if they are real. People believe that they are participating meaningfully in an intelligible universe and this meaning is given through the religion's cosmology or philosophy[16]. Geertz's definition is not, then, an absolute definition of what religion is in all times and places but a context-determined one. With my research, I am trying to explain what happens when people find themselves and grow up within two different sets of religious symbols embodied inside different cultural systems.

I consider culture as a public symbolic system, where man, according to his own personal needs – economic, mystical, psychological, or physical needs – can arbitrarily choose the symbols which at a precise moment are more able to solve a particular trouble or to overcome a particular situation. Of course, this arbitrariness is always linked to practical and pragmatic contingencies and to the very often stringent necessities that every man must face during his life. In other words, when a person meets a problem or a new situation, he can choose, within the public system of symbols, the symbols which, according to him, will offer better help in that particular situation. Culture indeed is also this continuous change, rearrangement, (re)semantization of symbols, made by each person throughout these daily personal choices. The case of the believers of the Taiwanese Catholic Church shows how these people live inside two different symbolic systems, and how they arbitrarily use both symbolic systems in order to interpret the events that all of us could meet every day. In other words, these persons become the space, the *jian* 間[17], where two cultures encounter one another and engage in dialogue. And the missionaries of the Catholic Church contribute to this dialogue. In order to translate their message and render it more understandable to Taiwanese people, they created new symbols or invested the old ones with new meanings (Chapter 5).

Within this book, the situation of the Catholic Church in Taiwan will be read as a symbolic system, the Catholic one, made and accommodated by (and at the same time maker of) centuries of history. When this symbolic system arrived in Taiwan, it encountered a pre-existing one, made and accommodated by centuries of a completely different history. Since I intend to stress the particular dialectical role of culture as a maker of/made

---

16. James Bishop, *Clifford Geertz – Religion as a "System of Symbols"*, February 2020, accessed March 9, 2022, https://jamesbishopblog.com/2020/02/08/clifford-geertz-religion-as-a-system-of-symbols/.

17. Like many Chinese characters, the character *jian* 間 expresses many meanings: between / among / space / interstice / separate. Here I use it in the meaning given to it by Nicolas Standaert (2002).

by history, in this work I will analyze in depth the complex history of this encounter. An encounter that is intrinsically dialectic, in which neither of the cultural systems can be considered dominant in absolute terms. When the Catholic Church arrived in Taiwan, it brought along centuries of discussions and disputes developed in Mainland China based on the deep contrasts between Jesuits and Dominicans. This long dispute is known also as the "Chinese Rites Controversy." The core of this controversy, which started in the 17th century was whether the ceremonies honoring Confucius and the family ancestors should have been considered superstition and thus incompatible with the Christian faith. The Jesuits believed that they probably could be tolerated within certain limits; the Dominicans and Franciscans took the opposite view and carried the issue to Rome. This issue ended only in the 20th century and contributed to interpreting the rites and the religions linked to them (Buddhism, Confucianism, Taoism, and Popular Religion) as pagan practices spreading superstition and idolatry.

At the same time, from the perspective of Chinese people, this historical process developed on the conviction of the totally foreign nature of Christianity. It may be useful to remember that by 1721, Rome's insistence that Chinese Catholics could not perform Confucian rituals led the emperor Kangxi to forbid Catholic teachings in the realm, though he later relented. Kangxi died in 1722, and the tensions continued under his son, the Yongzheng emperor, to whom non-institutional religions and heterodox religious groups were "alien" and accounted as *yangguizi* 洋鬼子, traditionally the foreign ghosts or devils, by the Han people[18]. This conception was reinforced by the hostile attitude of foreign countries toward the Chinese empire at the time of the Opium War. Therefore, since that time most Taiwanese people were already familiar with the negative interpretations of Christian symbols, and consequently, they considered the Dominican missionaries, who were the first missionaries to arrive on the island, as enemies and charlatans. This situation relegated the missionaries to the margins of Taiwanese society and strongly influenced the development of their evangelization process. Only after 1949, when many missionaries who were working in Mainland China moved to Taiwan, the Catholic Church was able to achieve a more central (and high) position within the fabric of Taiwanese society. Therefore, it is possible to find a very particular situation in Taiwan. A game played on the religious field where on the one hand we have a new cultural system that already provided interpretations of the dominant symbols of the local tradition as idols or heresy, and on the other hand, we have a local symbolic system that already approached the new in terms of barbaric consideration. As many people told me, a foreigner "ontologically" doesn't understand the existing cultural etiquette 老外不懂禮貌.

---

18. Eugenio Menegon, "Yongzheng's Conundrum. The Emperor on Christianity, Religions, and Heterodoxy," in *Rooted in Hope: China – Religion – Christianity*, ed. Barbara Hoster, Dirk Kuhlmann, and Wesolowski Zbigniew (Sankt Augustin: Institut Monumenta Serica, 2017), 311–335.

1 Introduction

The complexity of this situation helped to develop a great number of local variations which define the peculiarity of the Taiwanese Catholic Church. In order to better understand this process, I analyzed the historical processes which, as I already mentioned above, started with the dispute about the Chinese rites at the time of Matteo Ricci, and continued in Taiwan. Especially after 1949, an important number of missionaries, expelled from Mainland China, arrived in Taiwan, creating the actual administrative and historical situation that is still present today on the island. From the material I am going to introduce in the next chapters, the reader will learn how this historical encounter produced many local and particular situations. In order to understand how this historical encounter influenced the local situations, but without missing Ariadne's thread of research in the labyrinth of phenomenology, it is necessary to define some stable theoretical guidelines.

1.4.1 Historical Contacts

This kind of historical meeting, or the encounter of two different cultures, has been studied by many anthropologists, but I found the work of Sahlins[19] about the arrival of Captain Cook on the Hawaii Islands and the interpretation of this event made by the natives according to their own cultural structural schemes, more directly related to my study. Sahlins was the first anthropologist who started to consider the structure of the culture in order to understand a historical event. His analysis focuses on how the Hawaiians interpreted the arrival of Captain Cook using their cultural structures. According to Sahlins, Cook was considered a divinity – Lono – by the native people, and when the divinity created an existential crisis, with unexpected behavior, the Hawaiians determined that the divinity Cook should be killed, and sacrificed in order to preserve their cultural structures. In the final ritual inversion, which however reproduces the ultimate fate of Lono, Cook's body would be offered in sacrifice by the Hawaiian king. Cook was transformed from the initial position of the divine beneficiary of the sacrifice to the position of its victim[20]. The point of Sahlins is that because of this encounter, the cultural schemes of the natives changed. Therefore, we can consider Sahlins' structuralist view of culture as dynamic, the structure can change because it encounters a new event. This is Sahlins' conception of history: an endless series of changes in cultural structures. However, the peculiarity of my topic led me to associate the presence of Christianity in Taiwan with the reflections that George Simmel made about the "stranger"[21].

---

19. Marshall Sahlins, *Islands of History* (University of Chicago Press, 1985); Marshall Sahlins, *How "Natives" Think: About Captain Cook, For Example* (University of Chicago Press, October 1996).
20. Sahlins, *Islands of History*, 83.
21. Georg Simmel, "The Stranger," trans. Ramona Mosse, *The Baffler* 30, no. 30 (2016): 176–179.

> A stranger is not a wanderer, who may come today and leave tomorrow. He comes today – and stays. He is a potential wanderer: although he has not moved on from society, he has not quite shed the freedom to stay or go, either. He remains within a specific place, but he has not always belonged to it, and so he carries into it qualities that do not, could not, belong there. The stranger is a paradox: he is here, close at hand, but his having recently been far away is also present to us.

In other words, my research wants to deal with the question: what happens after the first encounter? What happens when the stranger who came yesterday will stay also tomorrow? In order to answer these questions, I found it very useful to read the book "The Conquest of America", by Todorov[22]. Todorov's book also deals with a situation of cultural contact, but it addresses it from a different perspective. In order to further analyze the encounter between an "I" and the "other," Todorov organized his work into four parts: Discovering, Conquest, Love, and Knowledge. By doing this, the Bulgarian scholar introduces us to the encounter between two different cultures, the Spaniard as representative of European civility and the Aztec one. From him, I borrowed the idea that this kind of encounter is in reality a process, and not a univocal and structural approach. This process involves in itself different ways to approach and relate the subject with the other. As we will see, Todorov tries to outline three moments or levels inside this encounter, levels which comprehend a first value of judgment on the basis of the subject's own culture, followed by another level, the identification of the subject with the values of the other or the imposition of the subject own image upon him. Finally, the subject can recognize the identity of the other and in this way, he can better understand his own identity.

1.5 *Jian* 間: Where History and Culture meet

The ancestors' rites in the Taiwanese Catholic Church must be considered as an encounter between two different cultural systems. I believe that this type of encounter between two different cultures cannot be considered other than a dialectical process. A process where the symbols are adapted by both the participants of this dialogue in order to try to interpret (Taiwanese) and communicate (missionaries) within the contingent events that everyday life brings with it. What the reader will learn in the next pages, is that cultures don't meet or clash, people meet or clash. Cultures meet and interact only through the intercession of people, through the use of words (spoken or written), expressions (verbal or facial), gestures, and activities. Therefore, it seems to me important to consider the persons who have come into

---

22. Tzvetan Todorov, *The conquest of America: the question of the other* (Norman: University of Oklahoma Press, 1999).

1 Introduction

contact with the two religious traditions and who, very often, coexist with these traditions, as a space where these two cultures encounter each other's and start to interact creating a dialogue made of agreements, contrasts, compromises, and choices. By considering the person as a space (a *jian* 間, as suggested by Standaert[23]), it is possible to understand how the encounter between these two cultures, which happened some centuries ago in China or some years ago in Taiwan, is still happening even today. Since this encounter was historical, it created a series of cultural interpretations (from both sides) that become immanent such as the concept of *doxa* described by Bourdieu[24], who uses the term *doxa* to denote a society's taken-for-granted, unquestioned truths. In other words, *doxa* is like a foundation of knowledge or beliefs. The historical encounter between the Catholic Church and the Taiwanese cultural context, thus, creates several *doxai* based on the negative interpretation and description of the other[25]. These *doxai* are immanent to the context formed by the encounter of a person with the new faith. It follows that within the space formed by the person, the three levels proposed by Todorov (judgment, rapprochement, and identification) are not only a process: different levels can coexist at the same time. They are not set once and for all, but each person still refers to them as changeable and re-interpretable concepts. Throughout their (re)interpretations problems and practices are faced and different local contexts are built. The ancestors, and consequently the ancestors' rites, are symbols which, in different ways, are embodied in both cultural systems, the Han and the Catholic one. Both religious cosmologies share the concept that life will not end with the death of the body, but the soul will continue to live. The fundamental divergence is that the Han popular religion cosmology shared the belief that each person has three souls (*hun* 魂) and seven spirits (*po* 魄). This is a very old concept, that probably dates back to before the arrival of Buddhism in China[26], people believed that after death one soul remains with the body in the grave; one takes residence in the ancestors' tablet; and one goes to the other world, usually to a purgatory. On the contrary, Catholic doctrine is based on the belief that each person has only one soul, which after this world will go to heaven or hell, or maybe in purgatory[27]. The Catholic soul does not continue to live in the same physical world as his descendants, and more importantly, the soul does not share their same physical needs.

---

23. Nicolas Standaert, "Contact between Cultures: The Case of Christianity in China (Some Methodological Issues)," in 輔仁大學第四屆漢學國際研討會「中國宗教研究：現況與展望」論文集, ed. Wesolowski Zbigniew (Taipei: Fujen University Press, 2002).

24. Pierre Bourdieu, *Raisons pratiques: sur la theorie de l'action* (Paris: Editions du Seuil, 1994).

25. Marco Lazzarotti, *Place, Alterity and Narration in a Taiwanese Catholic Village*, Asian Christianity in the Diaspora (Cham: Palgrave Macmillan, 2020).

26. Yu Ying-Shih 余英時, "中國古代死後世界觀的演變," in 中國思想傳統的現代詮釋, II (Taipei: 聯經出版事業公司, 1987).

27. Purgatory, from the Latin *purgatorium*, is, according to the belief of most Christian denominations (including the Roman Catholic Church and the Eastern Orthodox Churches), an intermediate state after physical death for expiatory purification.

This is a big difference between the two religions regarding the conception of ancestors: Han people believe that their ancestors still share the same physical and bodily needs. If these needs are not satisfied, if nobody continues to take care of the ancestors' tablet, the ancestors would cease to be an ancestor and would become a ghost, causing in this way many troubles for the descendants. On the other hand, the deep bond between these rites and the Confucian concept of *xiao* 孝, the principle of filial piety, represents a valid reason to allow these rites inside the Catholic Church, today as five hundred years ago at the time of Matteo Ricci. The need for the Church to be open to Confucian principles has been explained by Erik Zurker with his definition of "Cultural Imperative". He considers this cultural imperative as belonging to the deep structure of Chinese religious life in late imperial China. In the case of Christianity in China, he noted how no marginal religion penetrating from the outside could expect to take root in China (at least at a high social level) unless it conformed to a pattern that in late imperial times was more clearly defined than ever. Confucianism represented what is *zheng* 正 (orthodox) in a religious, ritual, social, and political sense. In order not to be branded as *xie* 邪 (heterodox) and be treated as a subversive sect, a marginal religion had to prove that it was on the side of *zheng*. The authority of Confucianism, and its sheer mass and attractive power, were such that any religious system from outside was caught in its field, and was bound to gravitate towards that center[28].

1.6 God, Jesus, and the Ancestors

In order to get a complete vision of this phenomenon, I tried to extend my work to different fronts, therefore I divided my work into seven chapters.

In the first chapter, I present a broad analysis of the works of anthropologists and other scholars who worked on ancestors-related topics. This overview will help the reader to obtain an exhaustive and complete knowledge of the ancestors' rites, and also of the relationships that link the ancestors with their descendants. Also, I will introduce here the relationships between the Taiwanese Han people and their supernatural beings: gods, ancestors, and ghosts. Ancestors are deeply linked with the otherworld conception of the cosmology of the Han popular religion, and these concepts are in some ways linked with the Confucian teaching about filial piety. These concepts influenced not only Catholicism but also other religions – Protestant Christianity and Buddhism – which came into contact with the Chinese world. The understanding of how these religions have addressed the phenomenon of the ancestors' rites will be a dedicated part of this chapter. This kind of research was necessary to me in order to better understand the interactions that mold the dialectic encounter between

---

28. Nicolas Standaert, "Matteo Ricci: Shaped by the Chinese," *China Heritage Quarterly* 23 (2010): 1–8.

1 Introduction

religions. After this analysis, I will consider the above-mentioned works of Sahlins and Todorov, which will be my starting point in order to understand the encounter between the two different systems of symbols.

The second chapter is more oriented toward the understanding of the historical background. As I showed above, I believe that the encounter of these two cultural systems in Taiwan was deeply mediated by the historical background, a history that started in China where some cultural symbols were created – the Catholic concept of Idols and the Chinese concept of *yangguizi* for example – and directly exported to Taiwan, where, because of particular historical events – the supremacy of Dominican missionaries, the hostility of the population, the Japanese colonization and the Second World War with its political, historical and social consequences – these symbols were elaborated and developed in a particular, local way, that created the situation today.

In the third chapter, I introduced the location of my fieldwork, the Resurrection Church in Wanhua District. This chapter will present some historical data about the church and about the congregation to which it is entrusted (The CICM, *Congregatio Immaculati Cordis Marie* in Latin, Immaculate Heart of Mary, *shengmushengxinhui* 聖母聖心會 in Chinese) and it will introduce the interviews I have taken with the parish priest and the parishioners. Some of the experiences of conversion of the faithful will be also described here. Moreover, I will introduce my methodology of fieldwork, explaining how to attend the everyday Mass gave me the possibility to know, through talks with the parishioner after the Mass, a vast quantity of information about other believers who don't attend the daily or the Sunday Mass. Of course, this work was integrated with and informed by interviews with priests of other churches, bishops, theologians, and especially parishioners of other churches. Especially relevant are the materials I collected during the month of November. November is the month traditionally dedicated by the Catholic Church to the deceased. Therefore, I visited other churches in the month of November. In this way, I saw how they prepared the ancestor's altar and how this kind of rite was performed. This collected material helped me to get a more complete and holistic view of this phenomenon.

The fourth chapter is based principally on the study and on the comparison of religious symbols. To give the reader an opportunity to better understand the implications of converting to Christianity, I will present some conversion experiences that have been told to me by those directly involved. Descriptions of the rites for ancestors performed in Catholic churches will be introduced, and through identifying the differences between the adjustment of these practices made by the Church and their original version, I will try to emphasize the profound significance of these changes.

The fifth chapter will introduce some of the key concepts to better understand the complexity of the Chinese People's Religion. Such as the concepts of time and *ling*. Through these concepts, it will be possible for me to describe the dialogical process that has formed – and at the same time shapes – the ancestor rites in the Taiwanese Catholic Church.

The sixth chapter focuses on the three categories in which most anthropologists agree on dividing the other-world entities of the Han popular religion: gods, ancestors, and ghosts. My study of these categories is addressed from the point of view of the Catholic faithful. According to my data, I tried to demonstrate that this structural division between these three categories is still real (also physically) for the Catholic people, and that consequently, these categories play a very important role inside the space (*jian* 間) represented by the individual.

Chapter 2

Anthropologists and Ancestors

2.1 A Brief Literature Review

Chinese ancestors' worship and the Chinese rites, in general, have aroused the interest of many eminent anthropologists and scholars. Since Freedman[1] and Francis Hsu[2], anthropologists have continuously and constantly researched and studied the relations between the Han people and their ancestors. In Taiwan, the research of the last past decades was performed by many distinguished anthropologists, including Ahern[3], Wolf[4], Feuchtwang[5], Harrel[6], Li Yih-Yuan[7], Wang Song-hsing[8]. These scholars' studies have already helped us to deeply comprehend the Han ancestors' worship phenomenon, and the relationships between ancestor worship and geomantic omen, lineage, kinship, family division, etc.

Freedman and his study about lineage organization could be considered as a starting point for the works of many anthropologists who, based on his theories, started to talk about "the relations between worshipers and the worshiped in the two contests of domestic and hall shrines; the rites performed in the two settings; and ideas about the roles of ancestors relevant to the two different contexts."[9] These spatial concepts, the domestic home, and the ancestral hall, elaborated by Freedman had become the basic point

---

1. Freedman, *Lineage Organization*.
2. Hsu, *Under the Ancestors' Shadow*.
3. Ahern, *The Cult of the Dead in a Chinese Village*.
4. Wolf, "Gods, ghosts, and ancestors."
5. Feuchtwang, "Domestic and communal worship in Taiwan."
6. Harrell, "The ancestors at home."
7. Li, "Chinese geomancy and ancestor worship."
8. Wang, "Ancestors proper and peripheral."
9. Freedman, *Lineage Organization*, 81–91.

for most of the research topics elaborated upon by many scholars during their fieldwork in the Taiwanese context.

Terms such as "domestic worship" and "hall worship", were elaborated upon by Wolf with the purpose of adopting the terms "domestic rites", "communal rites" and "corporate rites" to refer to worship ceremonies performed by one family, by a group of agnatically related families, and by the representatives of a lineage. Wolf also argued that the terms "home" and "hall" could then be reserved to refer to the buildings in which rites are performed. According to him, the placement of tablets also provides some evidence for his view that there are three types of ancestral altars: Domestic altars, Communal Altars, and Lineage shrines. The three types of altars reflect real differences in the nature of the three types of groups they serve[10]. Also, Harrel started to distinguish two points about ancestor worship. In his view Chinese ancestor worship is two separate cults: a series of rites that express the unity of a lineage or lineage segment (Freeman's "hall cult"), and a group of rites that continue the acts of filial obedience to recently deceased forebears (Freedman's "domestic cult" or "cult of immediate jural superior")[11]. Starting with this acknowledgment, Harrel focuses his point by trying to understand what happens to ancestor worship in a community where there are no lineages, where almost nobody owned the land until recently, and where an unusually large proportion of households contain members of two or more lines of descent. He argues that while the absence of lineages in Ploughshare has made ancestor worship a purely domestic cult, the lack of land ownership has helped to make ancestor worship much less closely connected with inheritance[12]. Another aspect of the ancestor cult in Ploughshare that perhaps connects with the natives' lack of property, is their failure to divide responsibility for the worship of different lines of ancestors. In many communities, the children of an uxorilocal marriage[13] are divided between their two parents' lines of descent, some taking the father's surname and worshiping his ancestors; others taking the mother's surname and worshiping hers.

He concluded that the question remains as to whether Ploughshare is an anomaly, possessing a type of ancestor cult found only in rural communities of wage laborers, or whether we might find similar situations elsewhere. Answering this question, Harrel agrees that the latter is much more likely; in areas of China where lineage organization was weak, in villages of fishermen, loggers, or salt workers, and even in poorer communities of farmers,

---

10. Arthur P Wolf, "Aspects of ancestor worship in northern Taiwan.," in *Ancestors* (The Hague; Paris: Mouton Publishers, 1976), 363.
11. Harrell, "The ancestors at home."
12. Harrell, 379.
13. From the Latin word uxor, meaning "wife," the English words "uxorial," "uxorious" (meaning "excessively fond of or submissive to a wife"), in the Chinese context it describes a marriage where the husband agrees to marry by "joining" his wife's family. The first or one of the sons will also take his wife's surname and not his own. Usually, this type of marriage is accepted by poor men, who could not provide a home for the future bride.

the order imposed on the ancestral cult by agnatic organization and patrilineal inheritance patterns were probably considerably modified in accordance with the local situation. In urban areas, where geographic mobility was greater and where affinal ties become more important among families of merchants, the strict patrilineal ideology might have been weakened and the ancestor cult accordingly modified[14].

According to Arthur Wolf and his famous piece "Gods, Ghosts, and Ancestors," the Taiwanese common people's point of view is that the character of the relationships that links the popular religion pantheon gods, is essentially bureaucratic (1974:133). For him "the Chinese supernatural through the eyes of the peasant is a detailed image of Chinese officialdom"[15]. The Chinese gods shared a clear hierarchy; a hierarchy that represents the Chinese imperial structure. For example, according to his fieldwork in Taiwan, Wolf considers Tudigong (土地公, one of the popular religion pantheon's divinities) a policeman for a community, and his roles are to spy on the affairs of his human charges, keep records of their activities and report regularly to his superiors[16]. In this way, people in Taiwan consider Tudigong as the lowest-ranking member of a supernatural bureaucracy, where Yuhuangdadi (玉皇大帝), the Pearly Emperor and Supreme Ruler, the mightiest god in the peasant's pantheon, is but a reflection of the human emperor[17].

The subject that the author presents in his concluding paragraph is very interesting. Wolf links the Chinese popular religion with the Imperial power in a very original way. Because he presents the Christian religion as a completely different symbolic system with respect to the Chinese local religions, this may explain the reason why the Christian religions are clearly and deeply considered by the Chinese – and Taiwanese – people as a foreign religion.

> In sum, what we see in looking at the Chinese supernatural through the eyes of the peasant is a detailed image of Chinese officialdom. This image allows us to assess the significance of the imperial bureaucracy from a new perspective. Historians and political scientists often emphasize the failure of most Chinese governments to effectively extend their authority to the local level. Certainly, many governments had difficulty collecting taxes, and some allowed this function and others to fall into the hands of opportunistic local leaders. Judged in terms of its administrative arrangements, the Chinese imperial government looks impotent. Assessed in terms of its long-range impact on the people, it appears to have been one of the most potent governments ever known, for it created a religion in its own image.

---

14. Harrell, "The ancestors at home," 384.
15. Wolf, "Gods, ghosts, and ancestors," 145.
16. Wolf, 134.
17. Wolf, 142.

Its firm grip on the popular imagination may be one reason the imperial government survived so long despite its many failings. Perhaps this is also the reason China's revolutionaries have so often organized their movements in terms of the concepts and symbols of such foreign faiths as Buddhism and Christianity. The native gods were so much a part of the establishment that they could not be turned against it[18].

The thesis that Chinese popular religion is in some ways linked to the imperial power structure has been expressed by other anthropologists. In his "Domestic and Communal Worship in Taiwan" Stephan Feuchtwang[19] describes the religious system reproduced in the annual round of Mountainstreet's domestic and communal ritual, and in a further step, he seeks to extract the selective definition of society that the system implies. Feuchtwang analyzes the three major categories of spiritual beings – ghosts, gods, and ancestors – which, according to him, are arranged in pairs of cross-cutting opposition, and puts these categories in the domestic/communal as an inside-outside concept. Putting all these in a calendar of contrast and continuity, he was able to assert that we find in the domestic and communal rituals of Mountainstreet three orders: a paradigmatic order of spatial contrast, a syntagmatic order of sequence and expense, and an order of inclusion. The first distinguishes the spiritual beings into several classes; the second establishes order and continuity between the classes; while the third arranges the classes as parts of even more inclusive categories[20].

His conclusion is that Chinese religion was a recreation of a metaphor, where gods are a metaphor for the system of authority, the state. The metaphor is one of the gods as rulers and judges and the mass of *gui* (鬼) as a beggar and supplicants being judged and saved by the gods. Yet *gui* are also a broken extension of the living into this domain. And though gods are neither *gui* nor ancestors, they and ancestors are placed in the same category (*shen* 神) and worshipped as insiders, in contrast with *gui*, worshipped as outsiders. Where god is to a locality like the imperial bureaucrat, a stranger with authority, and ancestor a native of the locality, *gui* is an unwelcome stranger and outcast native. This particular vision of Chinese religion as one "Imperial Metaphor"[21] was also supported by other eminent anthropologists, like Weller[22] and Ahern[23]. Ahern, in particular, defines popular religion as a game, and in playing this game Taiwanese people learn their social relations.

---

18. Wolf, "Gods, ghosts, and ancestors," 145.
19. Feuchtwang, "Domestic and communal worship in Taiwan."
20. Feuchtwang, 111.
21. Stephan Feuchtwang, *Popular religion in China: the imperial metaphor* (Richmond: Curzon, 2001).
22. Robert Weller, *Unities and Diversities in Chinese Religion* (University of Washington Press, 1983).
23. Emily Martin Ahern, *Chinese ritual and politics.* (Cambridge, etc.: Cambridge University Press, 1981).

2.1 A Brief Literature Review

Research about geomancy (*fengshui* 風水) and ancestor worship have been carried out by Freedman[24] and Li Yih-Yuan[25]. Freedman asserted that once a tomb was built, periodic rituals were carried out at the tomb site; the author has described the public, male-dominated nature of rituals surrounding tombs of apical ancestors, contrasting them with the domestic practice of ancestor veneration in which the female is the principal actor[26]. Fengshui ensures not only that the tomb is placed appropriately but also that it is safeguarded. In interlineal rivalry "the surest way to destroy a rival for good is to tear open his ancestral tomb and pulverize the bones they contain because the bones are decent; without them, one is cut off from the most powerful source of ancestral benefits"[27].

Li Yih-Yuan supports that inside these rites, the geomancy concerning the ancestor's tomb reflects the more affective, supportive, and rewarding-punitive relations of domestic life, while the ancestor worship in the tablets falls into the realm of a more formal jural authoritative relationship derived from the descent system[28]. The author explains the inextricable bonds existing between the family, the graves, and the ancestor tablets.

One other research front was explored in order to understand the boundaries of the three categories of supernatural beings, gods, ancestors, and ghosts. Wang[29], especially, stressed the fact that these three supernatural beings and their structural division reflect themselves in Taiwanese architecture. According to Wang, three different types of Taiwanese buildings – *miao* (廟, the temple), *sanmianbi* (三面壁, a particular temple dedicate to ghosts), and *zhengting* (正廳, the house living room) – express a fundamental division of all supernatural beings into three distinct types[30]. In a *miao* people worship the dead who have been deified as representations of legitimate authority; in a *sanmianbi* they propitiate the powerful dead who had served selfishly rather than for the community interest (see also 林瑋嬪)[31], and in their own *zhengting*, they worship the dead of their own line to whom they are obliged by descent.

Again, ancestors have been the object of analysis directed to understand their intrinsic nature. While Francis Hsu defines the ancestors of West Town (his fieldwork location in Yunnan 雲南 Mainland China) as "always benevolent, never malicious, and never offended by the descendants"[32],

---

24. Freedman, *Lineage Organization*; Maurice Freedman, *The Study of Chinese Society. Essays Selected and Introduced by G. William Skinner* (Stanford: Stanford University Press, 1979), accessed March 8, 2022.
25. Li, "Chinese geomancy and ancestor worship."
26. Freedman, *Lineage Organization*, 172.
27. Freedman, 139.
28. Li, "Chinese geomancy and ancestor worship," 332.
29. Sung-hsing Wang, "Taiwanese architecture and the supernatural," in *Religion and ritual in Chinese society* (Stanford: Stanford University Press, 1974).
30. Wang, 192.
31. 林瑋嬪Wei-ping Lin, "「鬼母找女婿」：鬼、三片壁、與貪婪的研究," 考古人類學刊 1, no. 75 (2011): 13–36.
32. Hsu, *Under the Ancestors' Shadow*, 213.

"ancestral spirit, in every part of China, are believed to be only a source of benevolence, never a source of punishment to their descendants. This is shown by the fact that when a Chinese is suffering some misfortune, such as sickness, fire, flood, or the lack of male progeny, he will suspect the fault lies with any of a variety of deities or ghosts, but never with the spirits of an ancestor"[33]. Ahern, on the contrary, supports the theory that ancestors direct their malicious effects toward descendants, and posits that people attribute serious illness and even death to their ancestors[34]. Ahern believes that the harsh child-training customs in Ch'inan (Sanxia 三峽, Taipei County, where she performed her fieldwork) were responsible for the highly malevolent activities of ancestors there. A painful experience in childhood throws a shadow over the rest of one's life, and the child expects that ancestors will behave in the same way as when they were alive. "The dead in the underworld retain the personalities while alive, but they are remembered as they were during their middle years, not as helpless old men and women awaiting death."[35]

Wolf arrives to define ancestors as ghosts if viewed from another family line viewpoint and also puts the emphasis on the tension between the good consideration of the ancestors and the fear of being punished[36]. "This seems to me only one manifestation of a conflict between an ideal that says the ancestors are always benevolent and a fear that they are in fact punitive. Asked if they believe that their ancestors would punish them for neglect, people usually insist that they would not. But when they suffer a series of misfortunes most people give serious consideration to the possibility that the ancestors are responsible."[37]

Wang classifies ancestors into two categories – those who are patrilineal forebears and those who are non-patrilineal kin, calling the former "proper ancestors" and the latter "peripheral ancestors."[38] This dichotomy is also a way to analyze the intrinsic nature of the ancestors. As we saw, most anthropologists who studied the popular religion phenomenon recognize a cultural and structural aspect of supernatural beings which is the division into gods, ancestors, and ghosts. According to my fieldwork and my experience in Taiwan, we can affirm that this way to divide these beings, and the structural relationships between them, is a basic concept among Taiwanese people. I would suggest that the most basic way to structure them in a schema, it is to consider the dead who have descendants who continue to pray (*bai* 拜) for them as ancestors, the dead who don't have descendants who take care and pray for them, will become ghosts. The dead prayed to by a multitude of people, not necessarily descendants, are considered gods.

33. Hsu, *Under the Ancestors' Shadow*, 45.
34. Ahern, *The Cult of the Dead in a Chinese Village*, 201.
35. Ahern, 218.
36. Wolf, "Gods, ghosts, and ancestors," 173.
37. Wolf, 165.
38. Wang, "Ancestors proper and peripheral," 365.

Every person must pray for his own ancestors, so it is necessary that every generation finds a way to preserve and continue the patrilineal descent system. Otherwise, the soul of the dead will cease to be an ancestor, becoming a ghost who will bring misfortunes and troubles to the family[39]. This concept is very important and as we will see, still influences Catholic believers' conversions and their approach to the new religion. Again, as suggested by the scholars mentioned above, there are two basic places where to perform the ancestors' rites; at home, and at the family hall. This point also stresses the importance of the *zhengting* inside the Chinese homes, and also – in the same way – the importance of the ancestor hall. These spatial concepts are also very important in order to better understand the way in which these rites are performed by the Catholic faithful, both at home and in the Church.

2.2 The Ancestors' Rites and the other imported Religions

Ancestors' rites have been a very important topic not only among the Catholic Church but for all the foreign religions, which tried, in different periods and different ways, to enter the Chinese world. With regard to the Christian faith, we can see that the reverence of ancestors is forbidden by most of the different Protestant Churches. Ancestor rites are seen as heresy because, in the Protestant doctrine, believers can only venerate Jesus Christ, the only mediator between God and humanity. According to this viewpoint, contrary to the Catholics, Protestants don't recognize and venerate the figure of the Blessed Virgin Mary or other Catholic traditional Saints. In the same way, they cannot venerate their ancestors, as these rites are considered a type of superstition, and the rites performed in front of the ancestor's shrine and tablets, are a type of idolatry. Anyway, if we analyze the history of Christian Protestant evangelization, even if it is not so easy to find a common background due to the conspicuous number of these different Churches, we can find interesting evidence of the great discussion of ancestor rites and worship within the Christian world[40]. Except for occasional references to ancestors' worship in the published books and reports of missionaries, nearly all of which condemn the rites as "idolatrous", the problem was not brought before the missionary public until 1877, after seventy years of Protestant work in China. The reason for this is twofold: the problem of ancestors' worship had not been recognized as a problem, and Protestant missionaries, acknowledging no central authority, had never met as one body until 1877. In his paper, Addison traces the development, between 1877 and the present, of the attitude of Protestant missionaries in

---

39. Lazzarotti, *Place, Alterity and Narration*, 105–106.
40. Addison, "Chinese Ancestor-Worship and Protestant Christianity."

China in regard to ancestors' worship. The significance of ancestors' worship in Chinese social life, and the problems raised thereby for missionaries are discussed, and it appears very clear how the decision to prohibit the ancestors' rites was long debated and hard for the Chinese.

The reverence for ancestors played an important role in the localization process of other religions in China. According to Weller[41] and other researchers such as Chun-Fang Yu[42], Erik Zürcher[43] or Stephen Teiser[44], every religion that has tried to enter China has changed its ideological core in order to adapt itself to the new cultural environment.

As it has been already discussed, today Buddhism is considered a Chinese religion, but historically, in order to enter and be accepted in China, Buddhism had to accept the worship of the ancestors. In the traditional Buddhist religion, (many would debate whether Buddhism could be considered a religion) there is no concept of the ancestor, so there is absolutely no need to venerate ancestors. The reincarnation theory basically eliminates the ancestor concept, because one's own ancestor – following the belief in the reincarnation cycle – may have already become an animal or another man or woman. Therefore, it would be completely useless to pray for or venerate ancestors. But now, even in the most important Taiwanese Buddhist temples, there are places dedicated to the ancestors. When the Buddhist tradition came into contact with Chinese cosmology, it needed to transform its ideological core to adapt itself to the new cultural environment[45]. Buddhism in China is, thus, a case of localization of religion[46].

Teiser[47], in his analysis of *yulanpenhui* (于蘭盆會), the "ghost festival" performed on the seventh month of the lunar calendar, at the time of the Tang dynasty[48], analyzed how Buddhist cultural elements were grounded in indigenous practices. According to him, the name *yulanpen* is usually taken to mean the bowl in which offerings are placed for monks, with the intention of rescuing one ancestor from the fate of "hanging upside down in Hell"[49]. The festival combined the interests of the monks, householders, and ancestors in an annual celebration of renewal. Most residents of the city, laypeople with no exclusive religious affiliation, provided for the salvation of their ancestors by making offerings to the monastic community.

---

41. Weller, *Unities and Diversities in Chinese Religion*.
42. Yu, *Kuan-yin: The Chinese Transformation of Avalokiteśvara*.
43. Erik Zurcher, *The Buddhist conquest of China: the spread of adaptation of Buddhism in Early Medieval China*, OCLC: 488646391 (Leiden: Brill, 2007).
44. Teiser, *The Ghost Festival in Medieval China*.
45. Weller, *Unities and Diversities in Chinese Religion*.
46. Zurcher, *The Buddhist conquest of China*.
47. Teiser, *The Ghost Festival in Medieval China*.
48. The Tang dynasty (唐朝) was an imperial dynasty of China that ruled from 618 to 907 AD, with an interregnum between 690 and 705. It was preceded by the Sui dynasty and followed by the Five Dynasties and Ten Kingdoms period.
49. Teiser, *The Ghost Festival in Medieval China*, 4.

Had the ghost festival been limited to a local cult phenomenon, it would hardly be known later in history. [Thus] Its ritual and material connection with the monastic community secured its place in Buddhist historiography, while its vital function in the ancestor's cult and the local community insured its survival into modern times[50].

Teiser stressed how these rites were adopted by the imperial power. The ancestral tablets of previous emperors, kept in the Imperial Ancestral Temple, were brought out, and offerings were made to them in bowls decorated with golden kingfisher feathers. In most years, after completing the ritual obligation for his ancestors, the emperor then joined in the festivities at the large temple in the city. The pervasiveness of the ghost festival in Chinese medieval society went well beyond the multifaceted ritual of renewal celebrated throughout the empire by the emperor and the common folk[51].

Other scholars such as Chun-Fang Yu[52] described this kind of religion's acculturation. The topic of this scholar was the localization process, analyzed through the transformation of the Buddhist Bodhisattva Avalokitesvara, a male figure in India, and in his earliest Chinese appearances, into the female divinity Guanyin (觀音). Chun-Fang Yu's work describes the process through which Buddhism became a Chinese religion. Using different methodological approaches, including analysis of Buddhist scriptures, miracle stories, pilgrims' accounts, popular literature, and monastic and local gazetteers – as well as images of Guanyin and the evolution of his/her aesthetic representation – Chun-Fang Yu stresses the particular role Guanyin has played in the process. Furthermore, by clarifying the dramatic transformation that saw the (male) Indian bodhisattva Avalokitesvara into the (female) Chinese Guanyin; or again the change of minor figure Avalokitevara into the universal savior and "Goddess of Mercy" worshiped by so many Chinese devotees; Chung-Fang implies that Guanyin is in a fact a Chinese creation[53], "Chinese created indigenous forms of Guanyin, just as they composed indigenous sutras" and further explains that "new forms of Guanyin appearing in devotees' visions of the Bodhisattva as contained in some later miracle tales served as effective media for the domestication and transformation of Guanyin"[54]. By "domestication" Chun-Fang Yu refers to the "creation of images of Guanyin unauthorized by scriptures" or with "no scriptural basis", aimed at presenting the goddess in a "way that would respond to the needs of the faithful"[55]. According to Batairwa the deep impact of this domestication could perhaps justify why most Chinese look at

---

50. Teiser, 5.
51. Teiser, 6.
52. Yu, *Kuan-yin: The Chinese Transformation of Avalokiteśvara*.
53. Batairwa, "What Do You Do When Visiting a Temple," 74.
54. Yu, *Kuan-yin: The Chinese Transformation of Avalokiteśvara*, 6.
55. Yu, 8.

Buddhism as a Chinese religion, forgetting the original atheistic orientation of Buddhism. The same process of metamorphosis has also shed light on the reason why during the first centuries, Buddhism was looked at as a special sect of Taoism. The reason will be simple, just as Taoism the "new religion" stressed the importance of meditation and encouraged a withdrawal from worldly affairs. Yet, the accommodation had introduced a radical component in the atheistic religion: Bodhisattva Guanyin was foremost a goddess, a savior to be worshiped and prayed and not only a role model to imitate[56].

The concept of ancestors not only resisted any effort of "religious colonization" but also caused an internal change, or at least a big debate, inside these religions. some scholars even believe it is possible to think of the rites of ancestors as a real religion[57]. In the next pages, I will try to show how the Han cultural system, and its internal structure based on the three supernatural categories described in many anthropological works, and especially the concepts of the ancestors, influenced Taiwanese Catholicism.

2.3 A Case of Cultural Encounter

I have introduced the idea that in order to understand the encounter between the Taiwanese cultural environment and the Catholic Church, it is necessary to analyze it as a contact between cultures. But what is culture? I believe that in some ways culture imposes meaning on the world; culture makes the world understandable through semiotic processes. "Believing, with Max Weber, that man is an animal suspended in webs of significance he himself has spun, I take culture to be those webs"[58]; webs of meaning which form every aspect of our daily life, from managing interpersonal relationships to the performance of daily actions, such as how to get dressed or what to eat. The concept of religion falls within the boundaries of this environment of meanings. Following Geertz, we can try to define religion as a cultural system, "where culture means a historically transmitted pattern of meanings embodied in symbols, a system of inherited conceptions expressed in symbolic forms by means of which men communicate, perpetuate and develop their knowledge about attitudes toward life"[59]. Meanings, according to this definition, are embodied in symbols and these symbols are historically transmitted. But because history cannot belong only to one person, it follows that these patterns of meaning also belong to a community, in other words, these patterns of meaning are public.

Religion develops and discloses itself known within the bounds of its own peculiar symbolic system, even though most people consider it only

---

56. Batairwa, "What Do You Do When Visiting a Temple," 76.
57. Paulin Kubuya Batairwa, *Meaning and Controversy within Chinese Ancestor Religion* (Cham: Springer, 2018).
58. Clifford Geertz, *Interpretation of Cultures: Selected Essays* (New York: Basic Books, 1973), 4.
59. Geertz, "The interpretation of cultures," 89.

as natural or supernatural. I do not dispute the natural or supernatural characteristics of religion, but we must consider and analyze religious phenomena as embodied in a specific cultural context. As Geertz reminds us, religious concepts spread beyond their specifically metaphysical contexts to provide a framework of general ideas of which a wide range of experiences–intellectual, emotional, moral–can be given meaningful forms[60]. According to these words, religion plays a very important role in the everyday life of people, giving everyone terms of judgment for the interpretation of life experiences, and for assigning them moral, intellectual, and emotional values.

Catholicism, entering Taiwan, brought a specific cosmology that was formed by centuries of experiences, ecumenical councils, and so on. As we will learn in the next chapter, when the Catholic Church arrived in Taiwan, it already carried with itself centuries of disputes and discussions about Chinese rites. Arriving in Taiwan, this religion met another cosmology, also built through different experiences and influenced by different political power, in other words, a different cosmology built through a different history.

Anthropologists like Sahlins[61] or other scholars like Todorov[62], even though in pursuit of a different purpose – and arriving at different conclusions – have studied events like this: the encounter of two different cultures. A brief introduction to the works of these authors will help an understanding of why I consider these authors important in the analysis of my data and my experiences in the field.

Sahlins' work helped me to highlight how the same event, filtered by different cultural frameworks, gives life to stories and to a different history for each participant in the meeting. In his book "Islands of History", he analyzes the encounter between Captain Cook, the great British navigator, and Hawaii's native people. An encounter, according to Sahlins, between a cultural structure[63] (the Hawaiian cultural structure), and an event, (the arrival of Captain Cook). Sahlins emphasizes the importance of the myth in this process because according to him and his structuralist conception of culture, it is through the myth that native people interpret contact with a foreigner and completely new entity. As Sahlins also stresses, Hawaiians were not the only Polynesian people to interpret the advent of early Europeans as a spiritual vision. New Guineans and Melanesians speak in terms of "ghosts", "ancestors", "demons", "goblins", "non-human spirits", "culture heroes", "mythical beings" or "gods", terms that according to Sahlins[64] could be found in an extensive literature ranging from first-hand accounts through personal recollections to long-standing oral tradition. The point is that the

---

60. Geertz, 123.
61. Sahlins, *Islands of History*.
62. Todorov, *The conquest of America*.
63. Sahlins, *Islands of History*, 103, 147.
64. Sahlins, *How "Natives" Think*, 177.

2 Anthropologists and Ancestors

natives interpret the intrusive coming of Europeans in ways consistent with the Hawaiian people's own cosmological schemes.

For a deeper understanding of this theory, although Sahlins' work is very famous, I am now going to give a short summary of it. According to the author, Captain Cook accidently arrived in the Hawaiian Islands, on the Kealakekua Bay, during a special ceremony, the Makahiki. The Makahiki was a ceremony that lasted four months and celebrated the annual revival of nature, where the central and most important event was the arrival of god Lono from his "house" on the sea, which was symbolized by one big tapa cloth and by a representation of a bird that was taken in processions in a clockwise direction around the island for one month. The Hawaiians used to divide the lunar year into two periods. One of them was the Makahiki time, during which the native priest of Kuali'l and the fertility god, Lono, peacefully regulated life, while the king was inactive. During the rest of the year, after the god Lono, turning away his bird's image, was gone again, a time of war came and the iimmigrant priest Nahulu and the virility god, Ku, were dominant, while the king was active again. Captain Cook arrived during the Makahiki, at a good time, from the right direction and in the right way. During the day procession, the sea was the principal taboo: no canoes were allowed to venture off. But because at the time Lono had arrived by sea, the people assumed that it was proper for them to go out to sea in their canoes; native Hawaiian people were convinced that Lono (Cook) was really a god (Akua) and his vessel was a temple (Helau)[65].

Because of this particularity and well-synchronized temporal conjunctures, the Hawaiians considered Cook as their god Lono. The captain was therefore consecrated as such by elaborate rituals in the big temple of the island, called Hikiau. After this, the Captain, who was exploring the Pacific Ocean with the goal of discovering the Northwest passage, again accidentally in accord with the Hawaiian calendar, left the island the same way he come. However, shortly after leaving the Big Island, the foremast of his ship, the Resolution, broke and the ships returned to Kealakekua Bay for repairs. But by sailing into the bay again on that particular day the great navigator was out of phase with the Hawaiian ritual cycle[66]. So, as Sahlins argued, the problem was not just empirical or practical, it was a cosmological problem, a situation that implied social and political problems: Cook's return in this season was sinister to the ruling chiefs because it presented a mirror image of Makahiki politics. Bringing the god ashore during the triumph of the king could reopen the whole issue of sovereignty[67]. The relations between the British and Hawaiian deteriorated, and then the natives took one of Cook's small boats. Cook, who did not want the natives to think they had an advantage over him, decided to use force.

---

65. Sahlins, *Islands of History*, 39.
66. Sahlins, 78.
67. Sahlins, 81.

2.3 A Case of Cultural Encounter

According to the native's point of view, this situation was no other than the god Lono (Cook) wading ashore with his warrior to confront the king[68]. In the final ritual inversion, which reproduces the ultimate fate of Lono, Cook's body would be offered in sacrifice by the Hawaiian king. Cook was transformed from the initial position of the divine beneficiary of the sacrifice to the position of its victim[69]. Following Sahlins, this transition from beneficiary to victim came suddenly, when the king started to perceive Cook as his mortal enemy. This explains how, when all social relations begin to change their signs, a structural crisis develops.

This is the history narrated by Sahlins, a concept of history that is made by a succession of changes in cultural structures or schemes. The changes happen when a structure meets with an event. Sahlins bases his theory on structure, event, and the structure of the conjuncture[70], he brings the structure into the historical process and creates a new way to interpret history. And this theory is, and I think that it will remain, his bigger contribution to the historical sciences.

Starting from another point of view, Tzvetan Todorov – a French-Bulgarian philosopher, one of the most influential voices in the European cultural world – in the book "The Conquest of America, The Discover of the Other"[71], analyzes the same topic, the encounter of two different cultures. As his book's title already shows us, the focus of his work is the "discovery of the other" as a process that is produced by the encounter between two different identities (persons, societies, cultures, etc.).

In this perspective, Todorov chooses a unique and exemplary historical moment: the discovery of America. This choice was dictated by many factors. First of all, at the time of this big discovery, European people already knew that other people inhabited their world, they already knew the existence of African peoples and in similar ways, they also already knew about the presence and of course the existence of Chinese and other Asian peoples. The discovery of America, for European people, represented the encounter with the "absolute other" with a real and in some ways inexplicable otherness. This theory was also endorsed by many scholars[72] who analyzed this aspect. According to their studies, at the time of the discovery of America, and most important of American Indians, a very big discussion was raised in Europe in order to define the nature of these people. If they really were men, consequentially they were also created by God because they were sons

---

68. Sahlins, 82.
69. Sahlins, 83.
70. Located between cultural expectations of what an event should look like, what, and how, it should mean, and how individuals exploit it for their own, historically meaningful, purposes, the "conjuncture" is the space where history is produced.
71. Todorov, *The conquest of America*.
72. Peter Hulme, "The Spontaneous Hand of Nature: Savagery, Colonialism, and the Enlightenment," in *The Enlightenment and its shadows*, ed. L. J. Jordanova (London ; New York: Routledge, 1990), 16–34; Margaret T Hodgen, *Early anthropology in the sixteenth and seventeenth centuries*. (Philadelphia: University of Pennsylvania Press, 1964).

of Adam; otherwise, if they were animals – like big apes – it meant that they could be considered slaves.

With the objective of analyzing the encounter between the self and the other[73], Todorov chose the history of the discovery of America not only because it was an example of an extreme and exemplary encounter, but also because according to him, it is in the fact the conquest of America that heralded and established the present identity of Europeans[74]. Analyzing the history of the conquest, Todorov's interest aroused several doubts in his mind about the conquest made by the Spaniards. Why Spaniards obtained so many lightning victories with a limited number of soldiers when the inhabitants of America were superior in number to their adversaries and fighting on their own territory? To confine ourselves to the conquest of Mexico, how are we to account for the fact that Cortes, leading a few hundred men, managed to seize the kingdom of Montezuma, who commanded several hundred thousand?[75]. The answer cannot be found if these facts are not examined within a cultural context.

As in the case of Captain Cook, Cortes was regarded as a god, Quetzalcoatl. This god is both a historical (a leader) and a legendary (a divinity) figure. At some moment in the past, he was forced to leave his kingdom and flee to the east (toward the Atlantic); he vanished, but according to certain versions of the myth, he promised to return someday to reclaim his kingdom. But Todorov's point is different from Sahlins's it does not establish itself on the myth to understand this kind of encounter. Rather the author analyzes how the Aztecan culture, basing itself on ritual and on divination and prophecies that were invariably based on memory because past and future were considered as the same thing[76] – produces a collision between a ritual world and a unique event. The effect of this collision was Montezuma's incapacity to produce appropriate and effective messages[77]. The Spanish invasion created a radically new, entirely unprecedented situation, in which the Spanish (but we could say "European") art of improvisation matters more than that of ritual[78].

Starting from these reflections, Todorov tries to give a cultural answer to these facts. Therefore, he divided the book in four important moments of the colonization process: Discovery, which concerns Columbus and the discovery of America, and in which the author analyzes the relationships between Columbus and the Indians and interprets the personage of Columbus in a hermeneutic way. The second part of the book is dedicated to the Conquest and to the greatest conqueror Cortes. In this part, the author analyzes the reasons behind the Spanish victory, putting in relief the differ-

---

73. Todorov, *The conquest of America*, 3.
74. Todorov, 5.
75. Todorov, 53.
76. Todorov, 85.
77. Todorov, 87.
78. Todorov, 87.

2.3 A Case of Cultural Encounter

ent ways in which Cortes and Montezuma – according to their own culture – interpreted the signs of the conquest. The third chapter is dedicated to the Love, represented by the personage of De las Casas, the first American Catholic Bishop. In this chapter, Todorov explains the meaning of terms like Take and Destroy, Equality and Inequality, Slavery, Colonialism, and Communication. The fourth chapter analyzes the Knowledge. Here the author gives us his typology of the relationships with the other and explains the importance of characters like the "mestizo" Duran and the phenomenon of the miscegenation of cultures. Finally, Todorov presents the work of the Spaniard Franciscan Sahagun as a way to understand the other. With this book, the Franciscan tried to acquire the knowledge of the other in order to realize his own objectives, in this case, the conversion of Indians.

According to Todorov, conquest, love and knowledge are autonomous and, in a sense, elementary forms of conduct[79]. Discovery is in another sense more linked with land than with man, and the main protagonist of the discovery, Columbus, is described only in negative terms: he does not love, does not know, and does not identify himself. By means of these three steps (discovery, as we have seen, is not taken into consideration by Todorov), the author builds his own pattern in order to understand the relations with the others. In this encounter, we can find three different kinds of typologies. First of all, there is the value judgment that Todorov calls the axiological level. At this level a person can recognize the nature of the other as good or bad, he loves or does not love him, the other is his equal or his inferior. A second typology is what Todorov calls the action of rapprochement or distancing, an action that the author describes as a praxeological level. That means that a person can accept and embrace the other's values, he may identify himself with the other or he identifies the other with himself and imposes his own image upon the other. Between these two extremes, there is also a third term, which is neutrality or even indifference. Thirdly, there is a third level, the epistemic one: a person knows or is ignorant of the other's identity, he recognizes the identity of the other and he is also able to better understand his own identity[80].

Of course, there are relations between these three levels, but no strict implications. A person can know very well and recognize the identity of a certain culture but this does not mean that he likes it. Or he may like it but he doesn't recognize the other's identity. Also here, as in the work of Sahlins, we meet the same focus: people use their own cultural views, their own cosmology in order to understand and interpret a new event. The next pages will demonstrate that also in Taiwan, at least from what I saw during my fieldwork, this kind of process happened, and it is – in some ways – still going on.

I generally agree with Sahlins and Todorov and their idea of considering culture as the most important element of interpretation that men use to

---
79. Todorov, 186.
80. Todorov, 185.

understand and receive a new event, although there are some small – but fundamental – differing points with which my position doesn't coincide.

First of all, I don't believe that we can define culture as a structure (even if dynamic), in my own view, culture is a more dynamic and creative entity. To consider culture as a structure means to lose a lot of different positions that – at the same time – live within the same cultural environment. Borrowing from the famous linguist Noam Chomsky's critique of structuralism[81], I also believe that structuralism loses sight of a fundamental problem: the creativity of language. According to Chomsky, in order to comprehend the functioning of a language, it is not enough to only understand its structure, as it is not enough to describe the components and the relationships between them, and it is also not enough to analyze and classify them.

Structuralism, according to Chomsky, cannot answer the question: "How is it that the speaker of a language is able to produce and understand an indefinite number of sentences that he has never heard first or that even can never be pronounced before by somebody?" Chomsky answers this question by claiming that innate creativity exists, which is governed by linguistic rules, and continuously produces new sentences. Creativity is considered one of the basic characteristic ways to use a language. While respecting the limited number of words and of existing rules, we are inclined to create something new that goes beyond the mechanical ways of the grammatical rules, even if the "something new" is in some ways generated by these rules.

Taking these ideas, thoughts back into context, one can suppose that even though we live in the same symbolic universe, it is possible that we assign two different meanings to the same symbol. This phenomenon happens because the symbols are the same, but the potential to interpret them or put them into relationships is infinite.

In the same way, I believe that the three steps suggested by Todorov are a process in which these steps are not fixed once and for all. What I mean is that in the moment of the encounter with the other, people can opt for and adopt one of the three points of view proposed by Todorov, and more importantly, they can change points of view according to their needs or with the contingencies of that moment, because of this the other can be my friend (and so accept the new faith), but I can change my mind and consider the other an enemy if the circumstances of my existence changed in the meantime. If culture is a public system of meanings, everybody who lives in the same cultural context can arbitrarily choose the meaning apt to interpret one specific event. Of course, this arbitrariness is always linked to each individual's personality, knowledge, situation, economic contingency, and so on. Arbitrariness is mediation, a negotiation between the public system of meanings and the particular conditions, the everyday life, and

---

81. Noam Chomsky, *Syntactic structures* [in English] (The Hague: Mouton, 1957); Noam Chomsky, *Cartesian linguistics: a chapter in the history of rationalist thought* (New York: Harper & Row, 1966); Noam Chomsky, *Topics in the theory of generative grammar.* (The Hague: Mouton, 1966).

the practical contingency of each man. In my view considering culture as a structure means losing most part of these "arbitrary choices" and in this way, we would consider history just as a "mythological product" of the ruling class (kings, priests, political parties, etc.).

The meaning of this could be found in another of Todorov's works, this time on Bakhtin[82]. Following Bakhtin, Todorov argues that in structuralism, there is but one subject: the scholar himself. Things are changed into notions (of variable abstraction); but the subject can never become a notion (he speaks and answers for himself)[83]. According to Bakhtin the importance of a language does not reside in the textual production but in the "utterance", and the most important feature of the utterance is dialogism, that is, its intertextual dimension[84].

2.4 Person as a *jian* 間: The Space where Cultures Meet

According to all we discussed above, it is possible to propound that history is not only arranged culturally, but history is a process that contains symbolic systems with internal contradictions. In this process, the mythical structure is important but just as important is the daily life, because if it is true that culture is dynamic and that history is a process, remember that for common people culture is something static and concrete, fixed in the everyday practices that a person has performed since childhood.

In my view, the point where this encounter takes place is the person. Considering the person as the space where this encounter takes place, where these two cultural systems play their game, cultural systems need to be understood only in order to understand the elements by which the person plays the game because the rules are arbitrarily chosen in accordance with the "needs and wants" of the person.

Sahlins' thesis that social communication is as much an empirical risk as a worldly reference, and that the effect of such risks can be radical innovation[85], is basically right. These risks should not be considered as risks, but rather as culture itself. As Gramsci[86] pointed out, in order to understand a structure, we must get a movement and its own contradictions; the contradictions are an integral part of the structure.

Stressing the concept that the person is a space, the anthropologist's goal will be to analyze the encounter in itself, in this way both protagonists of this encounter, the Han people and the Catholic missionaries would be

---

82. Tzvetan Todorov and Wlad Godzich, *Mikhail Bakhtin: the dialogical principle* (Minneapolis: University of Minnesota Press, 1984).
83. Todorov and Godzich, 21.
84. Todorov and Godzich, X.
85. Sahlins, *Islands of History*, X.
86. Antonio Gramsci, Valentino Gerratana, and Istituto Gramsci, *Quaderni del carcere* (Torino: G. Einaudi, 1975).

2 Anthropologists and Ancestors

considered as the anthropologist's other. In my view, Sahlins work tends to emphasize too much how the Hawaiians interpreted and responded to the event represented by the arrival of Captain Cook. The European symbolic system (or in other terms cultural structure) is not considered in terms that help us to better understand the Hawaiians' actions[87]. This is because the author – probably unconsciously – puts himself on the westerner's side.

In fact, the European actions don't need a deep and accurate description, such as the Hawaiian one, because their actions are considered purely common sense, something that everybody (who is European) can easily understand. This is, in my view, the critical issue that Obeyesekere[88] addresses in Sahlins' work (a critical issue with which I don't completely agree), because at the same time, Obeyesekere faces the same problem. If Sahlins' place is within the Western side, then Obeyesekere look only inside the native side and at the construction of their rationality[89]. It seems to me that these two scholars overemphasized "how the natives think" and did not emphasize enough the concrete, dialectical essence of this event.

---

87. Sahlins, *Islands of History*, 19–21.
88. Gananath Obeyesekere, *The Apotheosis of Captain Cook* (Princeton: Princeton University Press, 1992).
89. Obeyesekere, 60.

Chapter 3

Catholicism in Taiwan, History and Anthropology

3.1 The Chinese Rites Controversy

It is quite common, in many Taiwanese Catholic homes, to find ancestors' shrines (*Shen-an* 神案 and *Shen-kan* 神龕), or at least, pictures representing familial ancestors. During the Chinese New Year, Taiwanese Catholics burn incense and offer food and wine to the ancestors' tablets. This is considered a way of venerating the dead. Taiwanese Catholics, especially if newly converted, often wonder whether these traditional ancestor-veneration practices are compatible with the Catholic faith. It is a question with a history that has very deep roots, dating back four centuries, beginning in the time of Matteo Ricci with the so-called "Chinese Rites Controversy." The Chinese Rites Controversy erupted in the 17th Century and was not resolved until the 20th. The term "Chinese Rites" does not refer to any indigenous Chinese rituals, but to three specific customs. First, periodic ceremonies were performed in honor of Confucius, in temples or halls dedicated to the well-respected Chinese philosopher. Second, the veneration of the familial dead, a practice found in every social class and manifested by various forms of piety including prostration, incense burning, serving food, etc. Third, the missionary use of the terms *Tian* (天 heaven) and *Shang-di* (上帝 lord of heaven) to convey the Christian concept of God[1].

Contacts between the Chinese world and Catholic missionaries started very early, since Giovanni Montecorvino, a thirteenth-century Franciscan missionary introduced the Gospel to Mongol-ruled China. But it was 300 years later that the Jesuit Francis Xavier started to evangelize the Chinese people. During his mission work in India and Japan, he realized what kind

---

1. Dy Aristotle S.J. Chan, *Weaving a dream: reflections for Chinese-Filipino Catholics today* (Quezon City: Jesuit Communications, 2000).

of high regard these people had for China. He was already on his way to China when struck by illness, and he died on the island of Shangchuan, off the Chinese coast, in 1552.

In the same year, Matteo Ricci was born. Thirty years later, in 1582, he arrived in Macao from Goa where he was ordained as a priest. One year later Ricci, with one other Jesuit, Michele Ruggieri, entered China. If the Dominican friar, Gaspar da Cruz, was actually the first modern missionary to China, where he stayed but a short time, the Jesuits under Matteo Ricci were the first to give a solid basis to the missions in the Celestial Empire. Ricci, in spite of South Asia missionaries (Dominican and Franciscan who arrived in 1633, but were expelled from China four years later[2], was firmly persuaded that the Chinese culture was deeply linked with Confucian teaching and philosophy, so he decided that Christianity must be adapted to Chinese culture, otherwise, there would be no possibilities for the Catholic faith to be accepted in China. Because the relationship between power, society, and Confucian teaching was so deeply rooted, Ricci's understanding of the Chinese world was based on the conviction that the whole Chinese social system was governed by the observance of *xiao* (孝) or filial piety. In 1603 AD Ricci, as a superior of the Chinese mission, sanctioned an approval tolerating the rites where no clear hint of superstition existed. Ricci forbade prayers of petition and the burning of paper money but allowed the burning of incense and the offering of candles, flowers, and food. In the latter case, Ricci denied that the dead benefited from the food offered them, but allowed the practice because it was the Chinese way of caring for the dead, to act "as if the dead were living" (事死如事生).

As to the ceremonies in honor of Confucius, Ricci said:

> The real temple of the literati is that of Confucius...To that place at every new moon and full moon come the magistrates of the city, with the usual genuflections, and they light candles to him and place incense in the censer placed before the altar. [They do this] without reciting any prayers to him or asking anything of him, just as we said concerning their dead[3].

It is important to remember that Chinese literates did not accept any scholar who did not venerate Confucius[4]. For this reason, Ricci studied the Chinese classics, and there he discovered that "Confucianism was essentially compatible with Christianity, developing out of a context of monotheism

---

2. Brucker, Joseph, *Matteo Ricci*, The Catholic Encyclopedia. Nihil Obstat, November 1, 1908. Remy Lafort, S.T.D., Censor. Imprimatur. +John Cardinal Farley, New York, 1912, accessed March 9, 2022, http://www.newadvent.org/cathen/13034a.htm.
3. Mark D. Luttio, "The Chinese Rites Controversy (1603-1742): a Diachronic and Synchronic Approach," *Worship* 68 (1994): 293.
4. Motte, Joseph S.J., 天主教史 (Taizhong: Guanqi 光文化事業, 1964).

3.1 The Chinese Rites Controversy

and only later acquiring polytheistic accretions"[5]. Therefore, Confucianism could become the first step to Chinese people understanding Christianity, subsequently, missionaries could start to preach the Catholic faith.

In order to better understand how the controversy about Chinese Rites was relevant inside the Jesuits Order, we have to know that Ricci's successor, Longobardi, was of a different mind. Finally in 1628, when Emmanuel Diaz (Junior) was vice-provincial, a meeting was called to study the question, but no decision was reached[6].

In the 1630s, The Pope allowed the members of the other major religious orders to work in China. This decision was a political one because, in addition to different views about the religion of the Chinese, there was another cause of discord between the Jesuits and the Dominicans. The former were protected by Portugal and their protectors were at Macao. The latter were Spaniards, and they looked to Manila for support. Juan Baptista Morales, a Dominican missionary who had been in the Philippines, denounced the Jesuits to the bishop in Manila and submitted to the *Propaganda Fide* in Rome a series of seventeen propositions representing the questionable missionary practices of the Jesuits in China. Morales described the Confucian ceremonies and the ancestor cult as religious observances. Relying solely on Morales' testimony, Pope Innocent X issued a Decree in 1645 that prohibited Chinese Christians from participating in the Chinese rites.

Wanting their side of the story to be heard, the Jesuits sent their own representative, Martino Martini, to Rome. Martini explained to the theologians in Rome that the Chinese rites were civil and political in nature. They only seemed religious because religious terms like "altar" were used. He did not deny that the rites, in the course of time, had acquired a superstitious color, but in their pristine form, the rites were purely civil and political. Besides, the Jesuits made sure that Chinese Catholics did not participate in the superstitious portions of the rite. In 1656, the new Pope, Alexander VII allowed participation in the rites *Proud Exposita* (as explained)[7].

For the next fifty years, the Christian adaptation of the rites was practiced, though the members of the different religious orders (also of the same order) continued to debate among themselves. The next step was made on 26 March 1693, when Charles Maigrot, of the Missions Etrangères, vicar Apostolic of Fujian, issued a mandate condemning the Chinese Rites because according to him the description of the rites given by Martini was inaccurate. In 1700, the Jesuits in Beijing, in an effort to advance their cause in Rome, appealed to the emperor Kangxi (康熙) to obtain the authentic meaning of the rites. They wrote a petition describing the rites and added their own interpretation, and asked for the emperor's judgment as to whether their understanding was correct. The document says in part:

---

5. Luttio, "The Chinese Rites Controversy," 294.
6. Brucker, Joseph, *Matteo Ricci*.
7. Chan, *Weaving a dream*.

> Performance of the ceremony of sacrifice to the dead is a means of showing sincere affection for members of the family and thankful devotion to ancestors of the clan (...). It is not true that good luck and fortune are being sought thereby (...). The real purpose of it is that they shall not forget their relatives of the same clan, but shall keep them in memory forever and without end[8].

The emperor replied as follows:

> What is here written is very good, and is in harmony with the Great Way. To reverence Heaven, to serve ruler and parents, to be respectful towards teachers and elders – this is the code of all people of the empire. So this is correct, and there is no part that requires emendation[9].

The petition and the emperor's reply were sent to Rome, but instead of settling the question, the emperor's declaration was taken as an insult to the spiritual authority of the Pope[10]. In 1704, after several years of investigations, Pope Clement XI declared the rites as superstitious and prohibited Christians from participating in ceremonies in honor of Confucius and the ancestors. The declaration gained further when Clement XI issued a papal bull in 1715, *Ex Illa Die*, unequivocally condemning the Chinese rites:

> Pope Clement XI wishes to make the following facts permanently known to all the people in the world (...)
> I. The West calls Deus [God] the creator of Heaven, Earth, and everything in the universe. Since the word Deus does not sound right in the Chinese language, the Westerners in China and Chinese converts to Catholicism have used the term "Heavenly Lord" (Shangdi) for many years. From now on such terms as "Heaven" and "Shangdi" should not be used: Deus should be addressed as the Lord of Heaven, Earth, and everything in the universe. The tablet that bears the Chinese words "Reverence for Heaven" should not be allowed to hang inside a Catholic church and should be immediately taken down if already there.
> II. The spring and autumn worship of Confucius, together with the worship of ancestors, is not allowed among Catholic converts. It is not allowed even though the converts appear in the ritual as bystanders, because to be a bystander in this ritual is as pagan as to participate in it actively.

---

8. Luttio, "The Chinese Rites Controversy," 299.
9. Luttio, 299.
10. Chan, *Weaving a dream*.

III. Chinese officials and successful candidates in the metropolitan, provincial, or prefectural examinations, if they have been converted to Roman Catholicism, are not allowed to worship in Confucian temples on the first and fifteenth days of each month. The same prohibition is applicable to all the Chinese Catholics who, as officials, have recently arrived at their posts or who, as students, have recently passed the metropolitan, provincial, or prefectural examinations.

IV. No Chinese Catholics are allowed to worship ancestors in their familial temples.

V. Whether at home, in the cemetery, or during the time of a funeral, a Chinese Catholic is not allowed to perform the ritual of ancestor worship. He is not allowed to do so even if he is in company with non-Christians. Such a ritual is heathen in nature regardless of the circumstances.

Despite the above decisions, I have made it clear that other Chinese customs and traditions that can in no way be interpreted as heathen in nature should be allowed to continue among Chinese converts. The way the Chinese manage their households or govern their country should by no means be interfered with. As to exactly what customs should or should not be allowed to continue, the papal legate in China will make the necessary decisions. In the absence of the papal legate, the responsibility of making such decisions should rest with the head of the China mission and the Bishop of China. In short, customs and traditions that are not contradictory to Roman Catholicism will be allowed, while those that are clearly contradictory to it will not be tolerated under any circumstances[11].

The Kangxi emperor was not happy with Clement's decree and banned Christian missions in China.

> Reading this proclamation, I have concluded that Westerners are petty indeed. It is impossible to reason with them because they do not understand larger issues as we understand them in China. There is not a single Westerner versed in Chinese works, and their remarks are often incredible and ridiculous. To judge from this proclamation, their religion is no different from other small, bigoted sects of Buddhism or Taoism. I have never seen a document that contains so much nonsense. From now on, Westerners should not be allowed to preach in China, to avoid further trouble[12].

---

11. Dale A Johnson, *Searching for Jesus on the silk road.* [in English] (Lulu Com, 2013).
12. Dan J. Li, *China in Transition: 1517–1911* (New York: Van Nostrand Reinhold Company, 1969).

In 1742 Benedict XIV reiterated in his papal bull *Ex quo singulari* Clement XI's decree and settled the question until Pius XII. Benedict demanded that missionaries in China take an oath forbidding them to discuss the issue again. As a final declaration, the bull required all missionaries to China to take an oath of submission to the papal decree. The pledge was worded, in part, as follows:

> I, N (...) Missionary sent to China (...) will obey fully and faithfully the apostolic precept and command regarding the Rites and Ceremonies of China (...) and I will make every effort that this same obedience be rendered by all Chinese Christians (...) I will never allow the Rites and Ceremonies in China (...) to be put into practice by these same Christians (...) So may God help me and his Holy Apostles[13].

Rome, having spoken, no more could be said on the question, but it may be noted that the Bull *Ex quo singulari* was a terrible blow to the missions in China; there were fewer Christians than there formerly had been and none among the higher classes, as were the princes and mandarins of the court of Kangxi[14]. From 1742 until the 1930s, the Chinese rites controversy faded into the background as more momentous events took place in China. The periodic persecutions of the Chinese Christians, the suppression of the Society of Jesus in 1773, the Chinese war with Russia and Japan, the Boxer Rebellion, the First World War, and the Japanese aggression – all these took precedence over the Church's problems. In all this time, the decree of 1742 remained in effect, and every missionary who went to China had to take the oath against the Chinese rites[15].

In the 1930s, events elsewhere prompted Rome's reconsideration of the Chinese rites question. In 1932, some Catholic students at Sophia University in Tokyo refused to participate in ceremonies paying reverence to the country's war dead. These ceremonies were obligatory for all students. Furthermore, in 1932, the Japanese invaders of Manchuria made the reverence for Confucius obligatory on all citizens as a way of promoting civic unity[16]. This created a serious dilemma for Manchuria's native Catholics.

Both the Japanese and the Manchurian Catholics saw the government–imposed rites as contrary to the teachings of the Catholic religion. In both instances, Church authorities asked the ruling government whether the rites were religious or civil in nature. The Japanese government replied that the rites were civil manifestations of loyalty and had nothing to do with religion. Rome then issued separate decrees addressed to the Catholics of Japan and Manchuria, giving them permission to participate in the rites

---

13. Luttio, "The Chinese Rites Controversy," 303.
14. Brucker, Joseph, *Matteo Ricci*.
15. Chan, *Weaving a dream*.
16. Chan.

3.1 The Chinese Rites Controversy

without any qualms of conscience. Given these developments in Japan and *Manchuguo*, the *Propaganda Fide* in Rome decided that the same permissions should be granted to the Catholics in China, where the question of the rites first arose three hundred years earlier. Pope Pius XII issued an instruction, entitled *Plane compertum est*, which allowed Chinese Catholics to participate in civil ceremonies honoring Confucius and the familial dead. The instruction lays down the principle guiding the decision from Rome:

> It is abundantly clear that in the regions of the Orient some ceremonies, although they may have been involved with pagan rites in ancient times, have – with the changes in customs and thinking over the course of centuries – retained merely the civil significance of piety towards the ancestors or of love of the fatherland or of courtesy towards one's neighbors[17].

The 1939 instructions also lifted the obligation of all missionaries to take the oath against the Chinese rites. In practice, Catholics were permitted to be present at ceremonies in honor of Confucius in Confucian temples or in schools, and the erection of an image of Confucius or tablets with his name on them were permitted in Catholic schools. The Catholic magistrate and students were allowed to passively attend public ceremonies, which have the appearance of superstition. The instructions also assured that it was allowed to bow before the dead or their images. Ending the oath on the Chinese rites, which was prescribed by Benedict XIV, was considered not fully in accord with recent regulations and thus considered superfluous.

Despite the Church's sanctioned approval, the methodology of Matteo Ricci remained suspect until 1958, when Pope John XIII, by decree in his encyclical *Princeps Pastorum*, proposed that Ricci become "the model of missionaries." Around that time in Rome, the Council of Vatican II (1962–1965) was convoked. One of the principal topics of the Council emphasizes the noteworthy importance of bishops undertaking the appropriate implantation of the Church in other countries. It was only at that time that Catholics in China and in Taiwan were allowed to put the ancestor tablets and the ancestor altars in their homes.

3.1.1 Anthropological Considerations of the Chinese Rites Controversy

The first consideration that comes out from the reading of the Chinese Rites Controversy historical background, is it seems to me the Chinese people had no chance to participate in this discussion. In other words, the "problem" with Chinese rites was only a problem of Western missionaries. A problem

---

17. George Minamiki, *The Chinese rites controversy from its beginning to modern times* (Chicago: Loyola University Press, 1985), 197.

between the two souls of the Catholic Church, the one who wanted to acculturate to the new place and new environments, and the other, which argued that embracing a new religion means totally changing one's life[18]. Until Westerners raised the issue, the Chinese never saw the rites as contrary to their Christian faith. If not, they would have openly rejected the faith, and this has been the case in China, Japan, and elsewhere. The Chinese participated in the ancient rites because they were Chinese, and becoming Christians should not mean rejecting their Chineseness[19].

As we saw, during this long history of more than 400 years the same question was continuously asked: are the rites in their essence civil and political, or are they religious? If they are civil and political, they are permissible, if they are religious, they are prohibited. Starting from this consideration, I try to offer one other point of view, based on my personal experience in Taiwan but also partially advanced by other scholars[20].

It is my conviction that for western people the "Personal" dimension of religion became one foundation of the faith. This personal way to achieve the will or the union with God can also be found during the medieval period. Many religious orders, Benedictines, Cenobites, Cistercians, and Eremites – and particularly in the Anchorites in Africa – favor isolation from the world, because only by separating yourself from the outside and corrupt secular world, you can obtain salvation for your soul. This was, in most cases, the teaching of the Church until the Second Vatican Council.

Moreover, since Francis Bacon's famous aphorism "Knowledge is power" and Descartes's affirmation "Cogito Ergo Sum", the individual's primary activity is thinking. Great emphasis was placed on the rational thought processes, and the result of this is the refusal to bring together two different, and in this view conflicting, thought systems or ideologies.

According to Doumont[21], since the time of Pope Gelasius (around A.D. 500), a clear division between the priests' *auctoritas* and the king's *potestas* started. In other words, the division was a distinction between the secular political power and the spiritual Church's authority. This conception also can be found in the works of many medieval philosophers and thinkers, like the Italian Dante Alighieri and his "Doctrine of Two Suns" explained in his book *De Monarchia*, written around 1308-1318s[22]. As consequence, in the Western worldview, there is a clear distinction between the religious and the secular. An ideology has to be either religious or secular, but not both.

---

18. Motte, Joseph S.J., 天主教史.

19. Umberto Bresciani, "The Future of Christianity in China" [in en], *Quaderni del Centro Studi Asiatico* 1, no. 3 (2006): 109.

20. Chan, *Weaving a dream*; Luttio, "The Chinese Rites Controversy."

21. Louis Doumont, "A Modified View of our Origins: the Christian Beginnings of Modern Individualism," in *The Category of the Person: Anthropology, Philosophy, History*, Michael Carrithers, Steven Collins, Steven Lukes, eds (Cambridge: Cambridge University Press., 1985), 93–122.

22. Dante Alighieri, *The De monarchia of Dante Alighieri*, trans. Aurelia Henry (Cambridge: The Riverside Press, 1904).

On the other hand, Chinese people particularly stressed the "communitarian", the familial dimension (*jia-zu* 家族) of religious life. Communities are very much lay-oriented and have lay responsibilities; the familial community recognizes the important role of the women who are the transmitters of rituals and traditions within the inner, the *nei* 內 sphere of the family[23]. And the principal activity of this type of community is "doing", not thinking. There are not as clear distinctions in the West between sacred and profane, also because these terms are unquestionably Western concepts, built in a particular cultural context, and in this way useless in order to describe and analyze other cultural situations.

Therefore, while the Western ceremonies and rites need particular places – as a Church (where in the silence you can feel the presence of God), and especially need silence and concentration – Chinese ceremonies need just a place, which of course can be the temple, but often can be a big tent placed on the road (*ban-zhuo* 辦桌 or *bán-dòu* in Taiwanese) or just the house. And the Chinese prerogative of these rites is the communitarian and, more important, familial way to celebrate them. During the Chinese New Year; there are no particular liturgies or complicated rituals to follow by people. Although People just have to worship their ancestors and the deities on the familial altar, then they can enjoy the family lunch, the most important thing is that all the family has to be together at this time in order to honor the ancestors and reinforce the social relations of the family.

3.2 Catholicism in Taiwan

The island of Taiwan has been part of a territorial jurisdiction since 1514, when it was included in the diocese of Funchal, the capital of the Madeira Islands of Portugal. As a missionary jurisdiction, there was some organized Catholic activity on the island. In 1576, the first Chinese diocese was established in Macao and covered most of mainland China and Taiwan. From the 16th century through the 19th century, this diocese was divided several times. In chronological order, Taiwan belonged to the dioceses of Nanjin (南京) on 1660, Fujian (福建) in 1696, and Amoy /Xiamen (廈門) in 1883[24].

In 1913, the Apostolic Vicariate of the Island of Formosa (Taiwan) was established, being detached from the Diocese of Amoy. It was renamed Kaohsiung (高雄) in 1949. At the present time, the hierarchy consists of Taipei (台北) the Metropolitan Archdiocese since 1952, founded in 1949, Xinzhu (新竹) a Diocese founded in 1961 and Hualian (花蓮) founded a Diocese in 1963. Taizhong (台中) at the center of the island was founded as a diocese in 1962, on the southern part of the island there is Kaohsiung

---

23. Nicolas S.J. Standaert, "New Trends in the Historiography of Christianity in China," *The Catholic Historical Review* 83, no. 4 (1997): 573–613.
24. Beatrice K. F. Leung, "The Introduction," in *The Catholic Church in Taiwan: Birth, Growth and Development*, ed. Francis K.H. So, Beatrice K.F. Leung, and Ellen Mary Mylod, Christianity in Modern China (Singapore: Springer, 2018), 1–14.

(高雄) founded in 1913 and renamed and upgraded in 1949 and 1961, Jiayi (嘉義) diocese founded 1952 and Tainan (台南) founded in 1961[25].

In September 1951 the Papal Internuncio to China was expelled to Hong Kong. Since 1952, the Papal Internuncio has been stationed in Taiwan. Also, the ROC ambassador to the Holy See has provided the only permanent diplomatic link between China and the Holy See. In 1971 Pope Paul VI, changed the status of the internuncio of Taiwan, declaring that the Vatican's representative is only a Charge d'Affaire[26].

Analyzing the history of the Taiwanese Catholic Church, it is possible to divide it into four phases. The first Evangelization was under the Spanish occupation (1626-1642) until the destruction of the Catholic Church by the Dutch. The second Evangelization (1859-1895) was during the last years of the Manchu, and a third phase was under Japanese Rule (1895-1945). The fourth phase is from the end of WW2 until the present day.

3.2.1 The First Evangelization (1626-1642)

In 1624 The Audiencia of the Philippines sent a small expedition to Formosa. It was led by a Dominican, Fr. Bartolomeus Martinez. The ship was blown off course by a typhoon to Amoy (廈門), in Fujian, where it was repaired. The following year it departed from Amoy, and another typhoon propelled it to the shore of Formosa, to a place not far from Jilong (基隆). Martinez went ashore and investigated the region. He returned to Manila and communicated the information he gathered to Fernando de Silva, who in the meantime was appointed as Governor-General.

The next year de Silva sent a new expedition of 12 Chinese junks and 3 galleys to Formosa. On May 4, the flotilla landed at a cape, which was then called Gongliao (貢寮) and is now named Sandiaojiao (三貂角). The Spanish gave it the name San Diego or Santiago (Shanzhiyewo 山志耶我). From there they went northward up to the island of Tajilongyu (大雞籠嶼) which they called San Salvador (Shengsalumodou 聖撒律末都). Under the Japanese, its name was changed to Sheliaodao (社寮島), and now it is called Hepingdao (和平島)[27]. In San Salvador, the Spaniards built a church, which they consecrated to All the Saints (Todos los Santos). According to Chen[28], here still exists an old wall on the grounds of the shipbuilding yard. In this first period, the Spanish missionaries built a second Church for the Chinese of Jilongxian (基隆縣), dedicating it to the Blessed Virgin. However, this

---

25. GCatholic.org, *Catholic Church in Taiwan*, 2022, accessed March 9, 2022, http://www.gcatholic.org/dioceses/country/TW.htm.
26. Leung, "The Introduction."
27. Chen Jia-lu 陳嘉陸, *Tianzhujiao yibainian jianshi* 天主教一百年簡史 (Kaohsiung: Youying Press, 1960).
28. Chen Jia-lu 陳嘉陸.

3.2 Catholicism in Taiwan

Church was destroyed by a typhoon in 1630[29]. The same year a Dominican Brother salvaged the remaining material reused to build a small church for the aborigines in their village of Tapari (Tamoli 他墨里, Tamaoli 他毛里) in the north of Jinshan (金山).

Another Church was built in Danshui (淡水) in honor of Our Lady of the Holy Rosary, in 1632, and another was built in Jinbaoli (金包里), a village in the North of Jilong. In 1634, following the Spanish colonization of the island, the Dominican priests arrived in Yilang (宜蘭), where they built the church of Saint Laurentius and, near the coast, a monastery for the Fathers and a provisional church. At Santiago (Sandiaojiao 三貂角), the Spanish had constructed a small fort. Not far from this fortification, one Dominican Father built a church and stayed there to announce the faith to the Aborigines. The church was dedicated to San Domingo[30].

On April 2, 1633, Franciscans began coming to Taiwan. They stayed in Jilong and dedicated themselves to the work of the apostolate until they were able to sail to Japan. But a typhoon made them drift back to Taiwan, from where, in 1637, they departed for Japan once more. However, the foreign priests were persecuted in Japan, so they returned to Taiwan. One of them built a church with a monastery for the Franciscans, in order to do mission work there and to serve as a place of transit for China[31].

In 1638, the Governor General of Manila wanted to unite all the Spanish forces, to battle against the Moros of Mindanao. Therefore, he called back the defense troops of Danshui and let the fort be demolished. As a consequence, the Spanish administration and the existence of the Catholic Church in Taiwan came into danger. First, the natives wanted to take possession of the fort. But their attack was beaten back by the remaining guard. For this reason, they took revenge on the four churches at the border of the Danshui River; and demolished each one. It became impossible for the priests to continue living there in peace, and finally, they moved to the churches in Eastern Taiwan. The Spaniards neglected the defense of Taiwan more and more. Moreover, the chapter of the Dominicans decided in 1638, to serve only the churches of Danshui and San Salvador (Hepingdao 和平島), because of the lack of missionaries. A year later, Jinbaoli (金包里) got a resident priest, while San Salvador was abandoned.

In 1641, San Domingo and Jinbaoli were the only places left with the Dominicans, while one Franciscan Father served Jilong (基隆)[32]. On August 3, 1642, Danshui was attacked by a Dutch force and captured on August 24, 1642. Then they proceeded to Jilong, killed the Franciscan Father, and burned his church and monastery to the ground. The Dominicans lost

---

29. Study Note Verbiest, *Special Issue on the Catholic Church in Taiwan: 1626–1965*, vol. 16 (Taipei: Published occasionally by the China Program of the CICM SM Province, 2004).
30. Verbiest.
31. Verbiest.
32. Verbiest.

all their possessions in Taiwan; and had been forced to leave their 4000 Christian converts on Formosa. Already based in Tainan since 1624, Dutch East India Company merchants used Taiwan as a colonial trading center for goods shipped between Asia and Europe, while missionaries actively converted aborigines to their Protestant faith near Tainan. The Dutch, including their missionaries, were themselves driven out of Taiwan in 1662 by the Chinese Ming Dynasty loyalist and General Zheng Chenggong, who brought his forces to Taiwan during his war of resistance against the Manchu[33].

3.2.2 The Second Evangelization (1859-1895)

According to historians, in this period there were indescribable difficulties against which the Dominicans had to battle during the Manchu government. These difficulties were the greatest obstacle to the mission's progress. The missionaries had little defense. They were too far removed from Beijing, and being Spaniards, they did not like to call on the help of France, which had done a lot for the foundation of the Catholic Church in China. However, They called upon the Spanish consul of Amoy, which was of some help[34].

Of course, this situation was a consequence created by the war between China and European countries. In fact, since that time, the Chinese government and Chinese people considered Christianity as a foreign religion, imported by colonial powers through war and weapons.

Since 1706, the 45th year of Kangxi 康熙, Catholicism was no longer allowed in Taiwan, and not a single missionary had been stationed there. But in the second half of the 19h century, the mission of China underwent a great revolution. As a consequence of the struggle between China and European powers for the opening up of the country, the Treaty of Tianjin (天津) was concluded between France and China. According to Article 13 of this treaty, the Government of China granted permission to the Catholic missionaries to establish them on the island, and to preach and confess the Catholic religion there; and to the Chinese people, the freedom was given to make this religion their own[35]. Just as in continental China, several harbors in Taiwan were opened up for commerce with foreign countries: Dagou (打狗), Anping (安平), Danshui (淡水), and Jilong (基隆) became open for commerce abroad[36]. When informed of these actions, the Roman Catholic Church body the Congregation for the Propagation of the Faith immediately notified the Rev. Fr. Antonio Orge OP, Superior General of the Spanish Dominicans, and authorized him to let the Province of the Holy Rosary undertake the restoration of the Formosa mission. Father Orge sent word to

---

33. Government Information Office Republic of China, *Taiwan Yearbook 2006*, 1st edition (Taipei: the Government Information Office, 2006).

34. Verbiest, *Special Issue on the Catholic Church in Taiwan: 1626–1965*.

35. Treaties of Tianjin, *1858, Tianjin – France / china's external relations – a history*, March 2016, accessed March 9, 2022, https://web.archive.org/web/20160305022918/http://www.chinaforeignrelations.net/node/162.

36. Verbiest, *Special Issue on the Catholic Church in Taiwan: 1626–1965*.

3.2 Catholicism in Taiwan

Manila and, in a few weeks, Fr. Fernando Sainz was on his way to Formosa. Father Sainz left Manila in January 25 1859, and proceeded to Fujian where Fr. Angel Bofurull, a missionary in Amoy, was waiting to accompany him to Formosa[37]. With three Chinese catechists, the two priests set sail for the island and, on May 18, 1859, they reached the port of Dagou (打狗known nowadays as Kaohsiung 高雄). The two rented a house near the port and on the evening of May 22, they took over. They encountered a lot of problems with the local population; the two missionaries were held prisoner by the Mandarin of Pitao (today Fengshan 鳳山) and luckily were liberated by an Englishman opium trader.

Father Sainz wrote afterward: "After the humiliations, we endured at the hands of the Mandarins, and after accepting their false promises, we boarded the ship of the opium vendor who had saved us. We had to do this because my companion, Father Angel, had been totally unnerved by the ordeal we had gone through. He was really ill, so I decided to get him to return to Amoy. He left on June 7, and I was alone in Formosa"[38].

In Formosa, Father Sainz, alone and continuously in trouble, founded 1859 the first church in Qianjin (前金) dedicated to Our Lady of The Rosary. This provisionary building had to be replaced by a new church in 1860[39]. In 1860 other missionaries came from the Philippines and in 1863 a church was founded in Wanjin (萬金)[40].

In 1868 Fr. Sainz bought a piece of land in Tainan (台南), at that time the capital of Formosa, outside the city, and constructed there a house and a small temporary church. The people burned it down. Then the English immigrants in Tainan too became sick and tired of the persecution of the mandarins. The vice-consul of France, S. Gibson, protested to the Daotai (道台), the superior authority in Formosa, in Tainan. An English ship bombarded Tainan, until the Daotai asked for peace. He was punished 40,000 ounces of silver, of which 2,000 ounces was for the Catholic Church, for the burning of the three churches mentioned above[41].

After the intervention of the French vice-consul, the missionaries were directed to settle in Tainan. Father Sainz took advantage of this and sent two of his missionaries to the north to see about reviving the once-flourishing Catholic mission there. These two settled in Jilong and stayed there for a year. But the natives proved unresponsive to their teachings, and the two disappointed missionaries had no choice but to leave the place.

Sadly, they realized that the time had not yet come wherein the old mission of Jilong could be restored. Canadian Presbyterians had, already from 1863, settled in Taipei. They had many students. In 1883, a controversy

---
37. Chen Jia-lu 陳嘉陸, *Tianzhujiao yibainian jianshi* 天主教一百年簡史.
38. Verbiest, *Special Issue on the Catholic Church in Taiwan: 1626–1965*.
39. Verbiest.
40. Chen, I-Chun 陳怡君, "宗教經驗的召喚與祖先記憶的重塑：屏東萬金天主教徒的記憶、儀式與認同" [in zh] (PhD Thesis, 國立臺灣大學, January 2011).
41. Verbiest, *Special Issue on the Catholic Church in Taiwan: 1626–1965*.

arose among them, and a part of the Presbyterians left their denomination and went to the South. When they came to the Catholic mission, they asked the Catholic missionaries whether they wanted to go to Taipei[42].

One priest went and settled in the North-West of Taipei, in a place called Heshangzhou (和尚州). Difficulties with the Presbyterians were bound to come, and they soon did. But the missionary stood his ground; he came to the mission to have a look himself. He was welcomed with a great show by the Christians. New resistance came from the Presbyterians and from the Mandarins. The latter declared the contract of the sale of Heshangzhou invalid and forbade anyone to sell the ground to the Catholic Church. The Presbyterians came to Heshangzhou, to attack the Catholic Church in conferences, insult the Immaculate Virgin, etc. In June 1888, Fr. Arranz bought a piece of land with a building on it: a house of four rooms, which was used as a temporary church and residence[43]. At the same time, he started to evangelize the places around Taipei, founded a church in Dadaocheng (大稻埕), and rented a house in the city of Taipei (sited in Taiping street 太平街), but the place was not suitable, and the work stopped there. Also, the mission of Danshui (淡水) was met with hostility from the Presbyterians, and so was abandoned. Mission stations were founded in Nuannuan (暖暖) and Xinghuadian (興化店).

3.2.3 The Third Period (1895-1945)

Although the freedom of the missions under the Japanese regime was in a certain sense impeded, the brutalities, plundering, murders, and arsons, of which the Church had been so many times the victim under the Manchus, became a thing of the past. The Catholic Church could take deeper root. Although the missionaries had to abandon a few smaller stations, a lot of new ones came into being. It was under this regime that the mission of Taiwan was elevated to Apostolic Prefecture, on July 19, 1913, with Clemente Fernandez as Prefect Apostolic[44].

The Japanese favored the immigration of Japanese to Taiwan, who settled there in great numbers. Among them were a number of Catholics, and it became a great problem how to take pastoral care of them. It was difficult for these people to pray in one church together with the Chinese because the latter were used to singing their prayers out loud. For this reason, these Japanese Christians were neglected during the first years of the occupation[45]. Under Japanese domination, a church was founded in Taipei for Japanese Christians, in 1926. In 1940, there were 200 Japanese Catholics in Taipei. The Dominican Fathers started to expand their missionary work

---

42. Verbiest, *Special Issue on the Catholic Church in Taiwan: 1626–1965*.
43. Verbiest.
44. Acta Apostolicae Sedis, *Acta Apostolicae Sedis 1913-12-20: Vol 5 Iss 18* [in English], vol. 5 (Libreria Editrice Vaticana, 1913), 366–367, accessed March 8, 2022, http://archive.org/details/sim_acta-apostolicae-sedis_1913-12-20_5_18.
45. Verbiest, *Special Issue on the Catholic Church in Taiwan: 1626–1965*.

in northern Taiwan, building the church in a place called Xindianwei (新店尾). After the erection of the Prefecture Apostolic Church, the bishop at the time chose the church as his residence and cathedral.

In 1940 his parish had 600 Christians (now, after being rebuilt, this church is in Minshenglu 民生東路). At that time, the parish had two outside mission stations: Heshangzhou and Shiding (石碇), and a catechumenate in Xindian (新店). The missionaries built a church in Jilong, but the place was a military base, and that fact caused additional difficulties for the Catholic Church. Although the priest did his utmost to punctually follow the precepts of the Japanese, the military staff kept a severe check on every move and activity of the people, especially of the Catholics; the latter never got the sympathy of the military caste. For a long time, the Dominicans had been looking for an opportunity to found a mission in Xinzhu (新竹). However, it was extremely difficult to purchase a bit of land. Only in 1938 were they able to acquire sufficient land with a house to serve, for the time being, as church and residence. But WW2 prevented all further development[46]. In the 1920s, the Dominicans had decided to start a mission in Jiayi (嘉義), at first renting a house in the city and sending a catechist there. In 1934 Jiayi got a new church with a catechumenate. By 1941 there were 19 missionaries in Taiwan[47]. The war in 1941-1945 was a real disaster for the Church in Taiwan.

During World War II, the Japanese colonial government put Western Catholic missionaries under strict surveillance and forbade missionary work among the local people. The missionaries of Kaohsiung and Jilong, two Japanese military bases, were forced to leave the cities (Taiwan Yearbook 2006). Former Prefect Apostolic, Monsignor De la Hoz was replaced as Prefect Apostolic by a Japanese priest, Monsignor. Joseph Satowaki. On October 17, 1944, the Americans started bombing Taiwan. On May 31, 1945, the beautiful church that was erected in Taipei crumbled under the bombings, and the adjoining seminary and the residence of the missionary were severely damaged. Likewise, in Tainan, some mission property was destroyed. On September 2, 1945, Japan formally surrendered and the Japanese had to leave Taiwan, Msgr. Satowaki among them[48].

3.2.4 The Fourth Period

In 1945 Msgr. Satowaki had to leave Taiwan, and a new Prefect Apostolic had to be designated, at that time the whole island had 18 priests, 6 sisters, and 10,000 Christians. On March 5, 1948, the Prefect Apostolic changed

---
46. Verbiest.
47. Verbiest.
48. Verbiest.

again, that year Taiwan still had 14 Dominican Friars, 4 native priests, and 10 sisters, with 13,000 Christians[49].

The arrival of the troops of General Chiang Kai-shek (蔣中正), and the numerous refugees from the Mainland, made for a huge problem for the Prefect Apostolic. Nearly all of these people spoke the Chinese of North China. They did not know the Taiwanese language, while, at that time, all the missionaries in Taiwan spoke only Taiwanese. Among the Chinese refugees, there were 3,000 Christians. The solution came with the problem, because among the Mainland Chinese, there were Chinese priests.

Although many missionaries had left Mainland China by 1949, they did not dare to establish their missions in Taiwan; because they were not yet sure that the U.S.A. would defend the island in case the Communist Mainland Chinese attacked. Nevertheless, in June 1950, there were already 45 missionaries and a hundred sisters in Taiwan[50].

With the expulsion of all the foreign missionaries from China in 1950, Chinese priests and a few Chinese bishops escaped the persecution. Since so many people fled from the Communists in Mainland China many Congregations also came, and they started hospitals, schools, churches dispensaries, etc. Missionaries from China already knew Mandarin Chinese and were used to the Chinese lifestyle. Nevertheless, note that because so many people came from China at that time, one of the things that attracted many of them including those from Taiwan to go to Church was the Roman Catholic Charity Caritas help coming from the USA and distributed through the churches. At that time the people were so poor, they approached the church, not just to know the faith and churches became full. Many of the conversions were made without knowing almost anything about the faith, but there were so many who desired to be baptized each year.

In addition, the Church officials were very involved in politics. The bishops were with the Kuomintang government, and because of that, the Church received many privileges from the government[51]. According to a 1956 statistic, there were in Taiwan 306 foreign priests and 95 Chinese priests. Churches were built not only in the big cities but also in more important villages. Especially from 1955 to 1959, the number of followers increased from 48,000 to 182,000 people. In 1959 there were in Taiwan more than 300,000 Catholic Christians; one-third of them were aboriginal people or Chinese from the Mainland[52].

Taiwan was divided into two Church Prefectures on January 13, 1950, Msgr. Jose Arregui, became Prefect of Kaohsiung and Rev. Joseph Kuo was appointed Prefect of Taipei. The Taizhong Prefecture was established on October 6, 1950, and the American Rev. Willian F. Kupfer was appointed as its first Prefect on January 26, 1952. The Jiayi and Hualian Prefectures were

---
49. Verbiest, *Special Issue on the Catholic Church in Taiwan: 1626–1965*.
50. Verbiest.
51. Government Information Office Republic of China, *Taiwan Yearbook 2006*.
52. Motte, Joseph S.J., 天主教史.

established on August 7, 1952, and Msgr. Thomas Niu and Msgr. Andrew J. Verineux, M.E.P., were appointed Administrators respectively. On this same date, Taiwan became the 21st Chinese Ecclesiastical Province and Taipei an Archdiocese, with Msgr. Joseph Kuo (郭若石) as its Archbishop, being consecrated on October 26, 1952. When he resigned from this office on December 19, 1959, he was succeeded by Cardinal Tien Kengsin (田耕莘) as Administrator.

Soon afterward, seven dioceses were formed: the Taipei archdiocese, and the Xinzhu, Taizhong, Jiayi, Tainan, Kaohsiung, and Hualian dioceses. The Chinese Regional Bishops' Conference, the highest managing body of Catholic affairs in Taiwan, was established in Taipei in 1967. The conference is currently composed of seven incumbent bishops and is presided over by Archbishop Joseph Cheng (鄭再發), of the Archdiocese of Taipei. As of March 2006, there were 15 bishops, 726 priests, and 1,067 nuns serving 300,000 Catholics in Taiwan[53]. According to Cardinal Shan (interview for Fides)[54] "in Taiwan today we have over 600 priests, but 400 are elderly, and only a little more than 100 are under 60 years old."

It is interesting to note that only after the Second Vatican Council (1962–65) was the use of the Chinese language adopted for the Mass: According to the Council document *Sacrosantum Concilium* (solemnly promulgated by His Holiness Pope Paul VI on December 4, 1963):

> 1. Particular law remaining in force, the use of the Latin language is to be preserved in the Latin rites.
> 2. But since the use of the native mother tongue of other countries, whether in the Mass, the administration of the sacraments, or other parts of the liturgy, frequently may be of great advantage to the people, the limits of its employment may be extended. This will apply in the first place to the readings and directives, and to some of the prayers and chants, according to the regulations on this matter to be laid down separately in subsequent chapters.
> 3. These norms being observed, it is for the competent territorial ecclesiastical authority mentioned in Art. 22, 2, to decide whether, and to what extent, the vernacular language is to be used; their decrees are to be approved, that is, confirmed, by the Apostolic See. And, whenever it seems to be called for, this authority is to consult with bishops of neighboring regions which have the same language.
> 4. Translations from the Latin text into the native mother tongue of other countries intended for use in the liturgy must

---

53. Government Information Office Republic of China, *Taiwan Yearbook 2006*.
54. W. Meldrum, *A Cardinal Comes of Age* [in en], website, September 2005, accessed March 9, 2022, https://taiwantoday.tw/news.php?unit=20&post=24892.

be approved by the competent territorial ecclesiastical authority mentioned above[55].

The same document also discusses the Catholic Church acculturation challenge:

> Even in the liturgy, the Church has no wish to impose a rigid uniformity in matters which are not contrary to the faith or the good of the whole community; rather does Mother Church respect and foster the genius and talents of the various races and peoples. Anything in these peoples' way of life which is not indissolubly bound up with superstition and error she studies with sympathy and, if possible, preserves intact. Sometimes in fact she admits such things into the liturgy itself, so long as they harmonize with its true and authentic spirit[56]

Prompted by these declarations, the Holy Mass was celebrated in Chinese. The first Chinese Mass was celebrated by Msgr. Yu Ping during the Christmas period. The people answered in Chinese to the prayers and sang harmoniously in their own language[57]. After the Second Vatican Council declarations, Taiwanese people were also allowed to have in their homes the ancestor's altar with the ancestor's tablets.

3.3 Some Anthropological Considerations

The first consideration that arises from the reading of the history of the Taiwanese Catholic Church, is that before 1949 just a few missionaries were sent to Taiwan. Therefore, the evangelization of Taiwan was concentrated mostly on the aboriginal people, due to the difficulty for Spaniard missionaries to enter Chinese society[58]. Only after 1949, when many Christians from Mainland China came to Taiwan, and many people, as we saw above, received baptism in order to receive the Caritas' food aid sent by the USA. During my fieldwork, I met a lot of Catholics who admitted that "I grew up eating the priest's flour and drinking priest's milk powder" (*wo shi chi shen-fu de mian-fen, he shen-fu de niunaifen zhangdale* 我是吃神父的麵粉,喝神父的牛奶粉長大了). But aside from the food, other initiatives attracted Taiwanese people toward the Catholic religion. As Cardinal Shan – the Cardinal of Kaohsiung at the time of my fieldwork – spoke in one interview

---

55. Second Vatican Council Fathers, "Sacrosanctum concilium," in *Documents of the II Vatican Council*. (Vatican City: LEV, 1963).
56. Second Vatican Council Fathers.
57. Verbiest, *Special Issue on the Catholic Church in Taiwan: 1626–1965*.
58. Verbiest, *Special Issue on the Catholic Church in Taiwan: 1626–1965*; Government Information Office Republic of China, *Taiwan Yearbook 2006*.

for the Catholic magazine Fides[59], "The Island in the 1950s lacked education and medical facilities, so the Church responded by concentrating its efforts there. We established many schools–three universities, 27 high schools and 10 professional schools, 10 elementary schools," Shan says. "Altogether we have more than 50 schools in Taiwan".

Doing my fieldwork, I also discovered that at that time, many families were baptized, or let their children be baptized, because according to them "in this way the children can for free go to a Catholic school". Children were invited to take catechism classes. After every class, the priest put a stamp in their exercise book; with three stamps children could have a sack of flour.

According to Gramsci[60] the supremacy of one social group, is expressed in two ways: as domination (*Coazione*) and as "intellectual and moral direction" (*Consenso*). Gramsci's concept of hegemony is opposed, in the Prison Notebooks, to the idea of domination. Hegemony is established by a complex system of relationships and mediation. Hegemony is, in other words, an accomplished capacity of leading. In accordance with Gramsci's words, it is my deep conviction that the Catholic Church in Taiwan has never been a hegemonic power. Different from other places, Catholicism in Taiwan did not rely on foreign countries' power to enter the island. As a consequence, we cannot historically compare the situation of the Taiwanese Catholic Church with the situations of other places where Christianity entered with the help of a colonialist power (as in Latin America, the Philippines, some African countries, and China after the Opium Wars).

If we analyze the first arrival in Taiwan supported by Spaniard soldiers, we can see that the first missionaries' evangelization was directed to aboriginal people and a group of Chinese from Luzon, who had infringed the Spanish laws in the Philippines[61]. According to the Verbist Study Note[62], Cheng perhaps means the revolt of the Chinese in Manila in 1603.

When the Spaniard's soldiers left Taiwan, the missionaries' activities had undergone a brusque retrenchment, until their expulsion by the Dutch. But the Catholic missionaries' time in Taiwan was really too short to establish deep roots. So, in my view, we cannot speak about Church domination or Church power. Also in the 19th century, the French consul intervened by bombarding Tainan. It was to help the English immigrants who lived there (Verbist Study Note 2004); the scope of France consul was to help the opium traders, not to help the missionaries work. Similarly, someone could argue that the same kind of "constriction" had been effectually used by the Church after WW2, with the American Caritas aid[63]. Material goods have become a way to invite people to embrace the Catholic faith. But if we analyze this

---

59. Meldrum, *A Cardinal Comes of Age*.
60. Gramsci, Gerratana, and Istituto Gramsci, *Quaderni del carcere*.
61. Chen Jia-lu 陳嘉陸, *Tianzhujiao yibainian jianshi* 天主教一百年簡史.
62. Verbiest, *Special Issue on the Catholic Church in Taiwan: 1626–1965*.
63. *Caritas Internationalis* is a confederation of 162 Catholic relief, development and social service organizations operating in over 200 countries and territories worldwide.

historical event, we can say that in the period between the 1950 and the 1960 – although the Church was really in a "gold period"[64] – the number of Catholic believers in relation to Taiwan's population was a small percentage. According to a 1966 statistic, the Catholic Church counted 265,564 baptized and 46,672 catechumens, while there were more than 12,000,000 inhabitants in Taiwan[65].

The reactions of Taiwanese society, in particular the temples shamans, (the *Dáng-Kì, Ji-tong* 乩童 in Chinese) to this process of evangelization, should also be taken into consideration. During my fieldwork, some believers told me that when they started to attend catechism class, their parents, probably "educated" by the various *Dáng-Kì*, started to complain, claiming that if they became Catholic, they could not return to their home after death, because the priest would have taken away the heart from their body in order to produce aspirins[66].

Another Catholic told me that his parents had told him that the priest wants to baptize him with the intention to take away his soul. His parents believed that the souls of Taiwanese Catholics were carried to the USA, where they would have to work in order to produce nylon clothes.

Another case that I had gathered during my fieldwork was about a family that had received baptism in order to receive the American's Caritas aid. All the members of the family have become Catholic, with the exception of the first son, who still takes care of the ancestors' tablets.

One woman told me that in order to more easily obtain the Caritas aid, the father was baptized, but she and her sisters were not because her mother was persuaded that a Catholic woman could not easily get married.

These examples show a clear and concrete opposition to the process of evangelization, one active opposition made by the *Dáng-Kì*, and one symbolic opposition made by the Taiwanese cultural environment.

It is therefore possible to say that the Catholic Church in Taiwan had never been a hegemonic power, as in Europe. The Church entered Taiwan because it had been expelled from another place, so the Catholic Church arrived here without structures, without clear plans of evangelization. The Western way of thinking, the Cartesian one, which many times has been the platform for the evangelization experience, was never the dominant "discourse" in Taiwan, and thus never become hegemonic. Accordingly, it seems inappropriate to me to analyze the encounter between the Catholic Church and the Taiwanese population in terms of secular power, as proposed by

---

64. Motte, Joseph S.J., 天主教史.
65. Verbiest, *Special Issue on the Catholic Church in Taiwan: 1626–1965*.
66. Traditionally, the corpse at the time of death was to be placed whole, without any missing parts, in the main hall of the house. There, the body of the corpse was carefully prepared, made up, and dressed before being placed on a carpet. After that, a yellow cloth covered the face while a blue one covered the body. The meaning of the story told by the *Dáng-Kì* is that if the priest takes the heart of the deceased, his body will no longer be complete, so this will be a "bad death" and the soul of the deceased will turn into a ghost.

3.3 Some Anthropological Considerations

Asad[67]. The Catholic Church never became a source of secular or political power in Taiwan.

From another point of view, knowledge of the history of the Catholic Church in Taiwan seems necessary. As previously pointed out, the evangelization process in Taiwan at least until 1949, was linked only with the Dominican Order. This is very important because according to the history of the Chinese Rites Controversy, the Dominicans were totally against the ancestors' cult, considering the Taiwanese popular religion gods as idols of the pagan religion, decried by the Bible, or similar to the pantheon's divinity of ancient Greece and Rome.

This concept leads people to see "the other" as a foreign enemy or as a pagan heresy, deeply influenced the relationships between the two cultural systems, and created a dialogue based on preconceptions, misconceptions, misunderstanding, and mutual mistrust. This kind of dialogue is still present in modern Taiwanese society, and knowledge of historical background can help us to see these phenomena in a new light. For Taiwanese people who now live in the twenty-first century, Christianity is a religion made by foreigners and headed by foreigners. I met many youth people who started to develop some interest in the Catholic religion, but as one of them told me "my father doesn't agree because he told me that this is a foreigner thing that does not have any relationships with us [Taiwanese people]".

In the same way, it is not uncommon to find priests or other religious leaders who still complain about the "Taiwanese Idols" and about their believers who attend the rites of the Church even though they still go to the temple. Western missionaries (and, for that matter, Western-educated Chinese clergymen) viewed the pantheon of the popular Chinese religion as if it was the pagan religion of ancient Greece and Rome, or the religion of the heathen Canaanites described by the Biblical prophets[68]. It appears clear that both these ways to consider the other are full of bias and are intrinsically linked with a judgment value.

My point is that these phenomena must be put within a cultural context, but remember that this cultural context was made by a historical process that comprehends these kinds of preconceptions, misunderstanding and mutual mistrust. Only with a deep knowledge of the historical process, it is possible to understand and translate the symbols which embodied the religious practices and the everyday life of people.

---

67. Talal Asad, "Anthropological Conceptions of Religion: Reflections on Geertz," *Man* 18, no. 2 (1983): 237–259.
68. Bresciani, "The Future of Christianity in China," 109.

Chapter 4

Fieldwork

The aim of this chapter is to introduce the situation of Catholic believers as encountered in the urban context of Taipei City, where very often only one member of a family is Catholic, and where the relationship between Taiwanese people and the Catholic Church cannot be considered in a univocal way, but rather as a kind of dialog. A dialogue in which the two symbolic systems reciprocally use their own cultural view of religion – as the structural division between gods, ancestors, and ghosts and the biblical definition of idols – in order to understand each other.

4.1 Fieldwork Place

I carried out my fieldwork in the older district of Taipei, the Wanhua district (萬華), Méng-chià in Taiwanese. Taipei is the capital of the government in Taiwan and the island's largest city, located on the western bank of the Danshui River at the northern end of Taiwan Island. Taipei, which means "northern terrace" in Chinese, is the political, economic, cultural, and transport center of Taiwan. The city owes its prominence and growth to its designation as an administrative capital in 1894, a role that was enlarged in 1949 when the Kuomintang lost the Chinese civil war on mainland against the Communists and retreated to the island of Taiwan[1].

The spot where my fieldwork took place was the Resurrection church, a little parish established by the CICM missionary priests. The international religious missionary Institute, C.I.C.M. (*Congregatio Immaculati Cordis Mariae*, Congregation of the Immaculate Heart of Mary, *shengmushengxin-*

---

[1]. The Kuomintang (KMT), also referred to as the Guomindang, the Nationalist Party of China or the Chinese Nationalist Party, is a major political party in the Republic of China, initially on the Chinese mainland and then in Taiwan since 1949. It was the sole party in China during the Republican Era from 1928 to 1949, when most of the Chinese mainland was under its control. The party retreated from the mainland to Taiwan on 7 December 1949, following its defeat in the Chinese Civil War.

hui 聖母聖心會 in Chinese), is an international group of over 1,000 religious men dedicated totally and exclusively to the foreign missions of the Catholic Church. The Congregation of the Immaculate Heart of Mary (CICM) was founded in the year 1862 by Rev. Theophile Verbist (1823 – 1868), a Belgian diocesan priest. He was appointed as National Director of the Work of the Holy Childhood in 1860, and during this time he showed great dedication, with special concern for missionary work among Chinese people[2].

Between 1949 and 1954, 250 CICM missionaries were expelled from Mainland China. Two of them made a visit of exploration to Taiwan in order to prepare for a new mission on the island. After this first approach, four CICM missionaries left Genoa by ship in December 1954 and arrived in Jilong (基隆) in January 1955. Archbishop J. Kuo (郭若石) assigned to them the Wanhua District of Taipei. They started to study Taiwanese right away and opened the first little church on Xiyuan Road which was soon followed by two other small churches: Dapu Street and Dongyuan Street. Beyond these early initiatives, they established the parishes of Wanda Road (Holy Rosary Parish), St. Theresa Parish, Resurrection Parish (Dali Street), and Christ the Savior Parish (Liuzhou Street)[3]. In 1958 bishop A. Van Buggenhout started the first Catholic primary school in Taiwan: Guangren primary school (光仁國小), situated on Wanda road (萬大路) in the Wanhua district, next to the Holy Rosary Church. In 1965 CICM started Guangren Middle School in Banqiao (板橋). In that period many Catholic schools were built in Taiwan to give Catholic instruction to the children of the faithful. Most educators or teachers were priests or nuns, and as a believer told me, at that time, after the war the economic situation of many families was uncertain, and many parents felt that society was unsafe. In this situation, many of them considered Catholic kindergartens and schools to be safe places to leave their children while they were out to work[4].

In the 1970s, CICM initiated several centers for special education. First in Guangren Primary and Secondary School, and later in St. Theresa Parish. In the St. Theresa Parish, a kindergarten was opened next to the church, and an activities center for old people was opened in 2006. In 1972 CICM signed an agreement with the Taipei Archdiocese stating that most of its work and all the parishes would be transferred to the local Church. In 1988 CICM agreed with the Archdiocese to create the Guangren Foundation: an arrangement by which all the schools, centers of special education, and kindergartens were transferred to the Taipei Archdiocese.

It is important to note that the CICM missionaries worked particularly for the welfare of poor people. In line with this, CICM started the *Jingren* (敬人) Labor Center which had its center in the Resurrection Parish. This

---

2. D. Verhelst and Nestor Pycke, *C.I.C.M. Missionaries, Past and Present, 1862-1987: History of the Congregation of the Immaculate Heart of Mary (Scheut/Missionhurst)* (Leuven University Press, 1995).

3. Verbiest, *Special Issue on the Catholic Church in Taiwan: 1626–1965*.

4. Verbiest.

was a Catholic Church-based NGO working for the promotion of workers' involvement in labor health and safety issues. The center provided technical, material, and moral support to the labor unions and other workers' communities, in order to increase the health and safety awareness of the workers and improve existing working conditions. Because of financial problems, the center was closed on January 2006. The original functions of the Jingren center were transferred to the Taiwan Labor Information & Education Association (TLIEA) in Muzha (木柵), another district of Taipei. At the time of my research, no parishioners were involved in this kind of activity, two individuals – both non-Catholics – worked there. The situation Catholic centers like the Jingren center was not an isolated case. As many priests said to me, after the Second World War it was relatively easy to build schools or hospitals, partially because of the good relationship between the bishops (who came from Mainland China) and the Nationalist government. But in the 80s, when the Church started to care about foreigners and indigenous workers' rights while opposing the choices of government on the questions of abortion and the use of condoms, the relationships between the Catholic Church and the Taiwanese government gradually became colder. On the other hand, the economic development of the island made Taiwan famous in the world because of computer technologies. In fact, many priests said that European and American organizations did not consider Taiwan to be a developing country any longer. Therefore, the help missionaries used to receive from these organizations was now allocated to other countries.

Furthermore, the development of education and the quality of the schools and universities created a problem for the Catholic traditional education system. What I mean is that the priests and nuns were the teachers in their schools, but with the development of educational norms by the Taiwanese government, secular requirements of qualification and specialization for teachers cut off many priests and nuns from this type of apostolic work. As a priest told me, the problem now is that in most Catholic schools, teachers are not Catholics; therefore, it is very hard to do evangelization work inside these schools. The Resurrection church is situated on Dali Street, not far from the Huaxi (華西) night market (Fig. 1). The first church was built in 1957 and was completed by October of the same year. According to the parishioners and the priest who showed me some pictures, the first church was just a little house made of wood, just like all of the houses on Dali Street at that time. On December 15th of the same year, the first Mass was celebrated. The present church was built between 1977 and 1979, a five-floor building belonging entirely to the C.I.C.M congregation. On December 16th, 1979 the first Mass was celebrated inside the new church. I participated in the Resurrection church activities, Mass, pilgrimages, and other activities of the Parish in the period between my arrival in Taiwan in February 2003, and July 2007, when I moved out from my house in Wanhua district to a new home in Taipei County. And during this time, for various reasons, the Parish changed priests three times.

4 *Fieldwork*

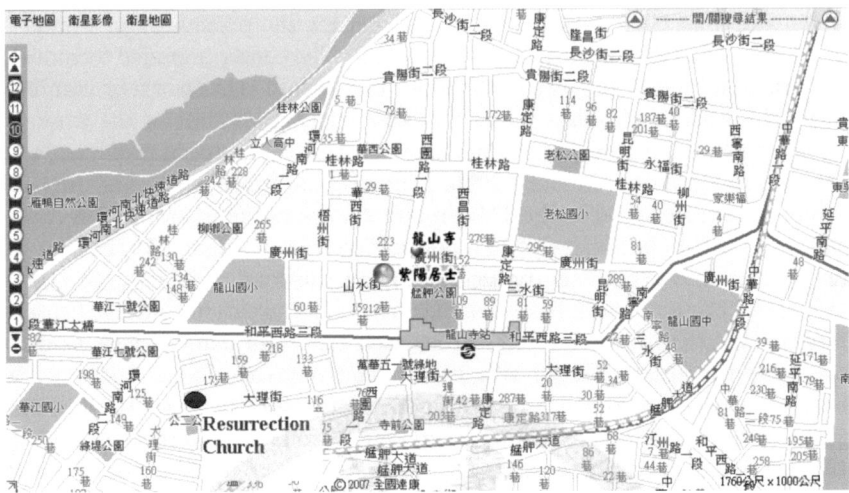

Figure 1: Location of the Resurrection Church

When I started my fieldwork, there were no priests specifically sent to take care of the Resurrection parish, but St. Teresa's priest – a bigger Parish in the neighborhood – was assigned to celebrate the Sunday Mass at the Resurrection church. Toward the end of my fieldwork, in March 2006, Father Martin, a C.I.C.M. Belgian priest who arrived in Taiwan almost thirty-five years before, was sent to take care of the Parish. Soon after Father Martin was nominated as parish priest of the church of Saint Theresa. In the Resurrection church, the Mass was celebrated only on Sunday mornings, while during weekdays there was no Mass because believers were used to going to the St. Theresa Parish which was only ten minutes on foot from the Resurrection Parish. According to the parish documents that Father Martin showed me, there were almost one hundred parishioners at the time of my research in the Resurrection church. However, during my fieldwork time, an average of thirty people came every Sunday to attend the Sunday Mass. Every Sunday most parishioners who attended the Mass were almost always the same, but sometimes new believers were coming in order to attend the liturgy, so during my year of fieldwork, I had met more than sixty people.

4.1.1 Who are the Faithful?

The definition of what is meant by the word "faithful" is another interesting topic. I once took part in a meeting for young Catholics. A friend of mine introduced himself in these words to a bishop who was present at that event: "Hello I am Chen Yizhang, I am not one of the faithful." (*wo bushi jiao-you*

我不是教友). The bishop, with the intention to let the young people relax replied: "No problem because the friend of a faithful is already a faithful" (*meiwenti, jiao-you de peng-you yi-jing shi jiao-you* 沒問題,教友的朋友已經是教友). By saying so, he was playing with the meaning of the Chinese word *you* (友), which can be used in relation with the term *jiao* (教), with the meaning of faithful, church member *jiao-you* (教友), or in relation to the term *peng* (朋), with the meaning of friend *peng-you* (朋友). At this point, a pedantic Religious Brother who was taking part in the conversation started to complain about the sentence said by the bishop and argued that, according to him, if the friend of a faithful person could be considered to be a faithful, the term faithful (*jiao-you* 教友) would lose its meaning. His argument was that, if things were such, people could be considered faithful (*jiao-you* 教友) without having received the Baptism.

The opposing views between these two religious persons is significant and most probably linked with the history of the Catholic Church in China described in the previous chapter. On the one hand, the bishop tried to be friendly and showed an open attitude toward youth and non-Catholic people, without stressing the rules or the importance of the sacraments. On the other hand, the Religious Brother stands in a completely different position: it is vital to preserve the identity of the Roman Catholic Church in the complex contact and dialogue with non-Catholics.

After this experience, I met another one of the faithful, a 40 years old man, who told me that when he received the Baptism, he first attended catechism classes in a parish where the priest told him that only after one year (at least) of catechism he could be baptized. This faithful person then went to another parish where the priest immediately baptized him. In fact, different ways and approaches by priests can be found in different parishes, which show that different and sometimes contradictory positions can coexist within the Catholic world, or using Todorov's expression[5], different levels of relationship with "the other" are implemented by the Catholic hierarchy in order to carry out their evangelization process. There is no uniform way to manage these relationships with "the other", this fact is linked with the complex and diverse process that both makes and informs the local expression of the Universal Church[6].

The above-mentioned situation can be found within the Resurrection church. In fact, through the investigation of the believers' experiences and memories, it is possible to learn that the approaches used by the different priests who worked there as parish priest sometimes differed significantly. For instance, when the church was built the priest invited children and adults to participate in catechism class, giving flour and milk powder, and the believers were baptized without a deep knowledge of the Catholic sacraments, rules, etc. The priests who followed started to do work of a different nature; namely, to train the faithful to become catechists and work actively

---

5. Todorov, *The conquest of America*.
6. *Catholĭcus*, from the Greek, means "universal".

within the scope of the Church activities. During the four years of my participation in these activities, I was able to note differences between the behavior and the habitual practices and techniques of the priests who took care of the parish at this time.

Some priests stressed the importance of personal visits to the faithful at home; some others stressed the participation of the faithful in Church activities, etc. I based my research upon considering people who were baptized – according to the parish registries – as believers. Most of the Resurrection church's faithful were baptized between the end of the Second World War and the 1960s, when - thanks to the significant material from the American charity Caritas, administered by the Catholic Church – many Taiwanese people were converted.

4.1.2 Experiences of Conversion

The examples of conversion which will follow have been collected during my fieldwork. They will help to bring into focus the above-mentioned concepts.

Miss Wu is the fifth of six brothers and sisters, the first is a male. She was born in Lugan, in central Taiwan. During her childhood, in the years following the war, her family was destitute, they were reduced to eating the flour and milk powder offered by the priest (*wo shi chi shen-fu de mian-fen, he shen-fu de niunaifen zhangda* 我是吃神父的麵粉和牛奶粉長大). And that time clothes were provided by the American Caritas. The priest naturally hoped that someone from her family would be baptized, but her mother was afraid that a Catholic woman could not easily find a husband and get married, so she convinced her husband to receive Baptism. However, after he was baptized, her father never went to Church. When she studied at university, she felt freer. She frequented the courses of a Catholic University in Taizhong. However, she attended some meetings with Protestant Christians that, according to her, do their apostolic work better than Catholics. But their approach was too rapid for her: after two meetings they asked her to be baptized, but she didn't want to because she felt forced, and then refused. The third time when people asked: "Who wants to become a Christian? Who wants to receive Baptism?" she didn't answer. Shortly after, she stopped going to these meetings.

After her graduation, she moved to Taipei for work. In that period, she reestablished contact with some Catholics. At that time, she was deeply touched by the visit of Mother Teresa of Calcutta in Taiwan. She felt attracted by the charisma of Mother Theresa and she understood that Mother Teresa's spiritual and moral strength came from her faith. Miss Wu felt deeply touched by this (*hen gandong* 很感動). After this, she started to attend classes in catechism, and although she did not know much yet about the Catholic faith, she decided to receive Baptism. Shortly after she had the opportunity to go to France for six months with a Catholic association. When she returned to Taipei, she started to take courses in theology, to better understand her own new faith. The point that she stressed continuously during our conversation was that she felt that within the Catholic Church she had found her family, a global — thanks to her experience in France -– and multicultural family.

Miss Wu was persuaded that even if she was baptized, she still respected her parent (*wo hai zunjing wo fumu* 我還尊敬我父母), because when she was baptized her father had already passed away and her mother agreed with her because Miss Wu's mother knew that Catholics were good people who helped them when they were in need and poor. Now, during every Spring Festival and Mid-Autumn Festival, she still returns to her hometown in Lugan, where she uses incense sticks to pray for her parents, but she doesn't pray for the gods in the shrine of the ancestors, her relatives know it and they don't force to her to do this.

As I pointed out before, except for two families who are traditionally Catholic – which means they were converted before the Second World War by the Spaniard Dominican Fathers – other families or persons were converted after the war and, as the conversion of Miss Wu's father, these conversions are indisputably connected to the Caritas charity help. These causes have played a role in the conversion of the most faithful of the Resurrection Parrish. Some of them were "converted" by their parents because in this way it was easier to obtain material help as well as scholarly instruction. Mister Zhang told me that his mother brought him to the Church because she was afraid for his future. The family was very poor and letting the child become a Catholic allowed him to get good education at school.

When I asked Miss Lin if there were other members of her family who were Catholics, she told me that only she was baptized. And when I asked her why she received Baptism, she told me that it was because her mother had wished it, but that she did not know the reasons which caused her mother to take this kind of decision.

Miss Li was baptized with her sisters and parents in order to receive Caritas' help and go to the Catholic school for free. She told me an interesting fact that can help with understanding how the cultural dialogue between two cultures plays in many different ways and on different levels. She told me that the whole family was baptized with the exception of her elder brother, who now takes care of the ancestors' tablets. On one level, the parents of Miss Li decided to baptize the whole family because of the particular needs of that time. At the same time, they have consciously chosen not to baptize their first child, who according to tradition must look after the tablets of the ancestors, preventing them from becoming hungry ghosts that will wander aimlessly for all eternity.

Thus, especially in the 1960s, the benefit from schools and hospitals was a good motivation for many Taiwanese people to embrace the Catholic religion. But nowadays circumstances are different. The Taiwanese Catholic Church is a big and complex structure, a body that contains many different experiences. It can happen that people embrace the new faith because of material needs or interest as shown by the above experiences; many young people who were coming every Sunday to the Holy Mass, for example, were attracted by the guitar lessons that a faithful organized after the Mass.

Nevertheless, according to the interviews that I made with some faithful, there is a significant number of other reasons behind the decision to convert to Christianity: a woman started to take classes in catechism because she dreamed of a Western man with long hair and a beard, and shortly after she discovered that the man who appeared to her in dreams was Jesus. Another woman told me that she was seriously sick when she dreamed of a woman who told her that she was the Blessed Virgin Mary and that if she would be baptized, she would recover from her sickness. She agreed, but her father did not let her receive the Baptism. However, she fell ill again, and at this point, her father agreed to let her be baptized.

It seems to me that the experiences of conversion have different origins than in the past: they are motivated by other kinds of needs, not material anymore, but psychological and social. As a priest told me, in Taipei people live under constant and significant pressure mainly caused by work, academic expectations, family relationships, and so on. Looking for a way out, people are often touched by someone, say a work colleague, a neighbor, or a classmate who is Catholic, and so they initiate contact with the Church. Most of the people that I interviewed told me that they were deeply touched by the fact that most of the Catholics that they met in their life were good people (*Wo ganjue dao tianzhujiao tu shi haoren* 我感覺到天主教徒是好人), maybe these individuals have been helped by these Catholic friends or may have been invited to some meetings or activities where they felt understood and accepted.

Miss Zhang was a fifty-year-old faithful. When she was around forty-five, she became deeply depressed, and because of this, she lost her job. At that time, she met some Christian believers who invited her to participate in their activities and after a little time asked her to be baptized. But her family opposed her choice and would not allow her to receive Baptism. At that point her physical and psychological conditions became worse, therefore her family allowed her to receive Baptism, within the Catholic Church, because Catholics are allowed to continue praying (*bai* 拜) to their ancestors.

As I noted above, most of these faithful live in a family context where only they are baptized, while the rest of the family does not have any relationship with the Catholic Church. Other believers registered at the parish were baptized, but they were not accustomed to attending the Sunday liturgy for several reasons: some of them were too old and there was nobody who could bring them to church, or sometimes because the husband did not allow the wife to go to Church, or never joined the activities of the Church after being baptized because they were too busy (*Tai-mang* 太忙). The parish priest told me that even the former mayor of Taipei city and former president of Taiwan, 馬英九 Ma Ying-jeou[7] was baptized in the old Resurrection church on Dali Street. He is the most eminent case of a believer who does not participate in Church activities.

Except for a few family groups and some young people, women represent the majority of believers. This situation is not peculiar to the Resurrection church, in every parish, the involvement of women in Church activities is more important than that of men. This type of situation generates a particular phenomenon. Where, very often, only one member of the family – the wife or the daughter – is Catholic, while the other members remain involved in Popular Religion practices[8]. Yet these Catholic women must participate with the rest of the family in all the rites, and practices that any believer of Taiwanese popular religion has to perform.

It is within this environment and context that I conducted my research. My fieldwork documents include several interviews with Parish priests and believers from other parishes. Through active participation in the Church rituals and interviews with the parishioners, through visits to their homes, and interviews with priests and theologians, I collected a significant number of ethnographic materials that I will present in the next pages.

4.2 The Taiwanese Catholic Ancestors' Rites

As already described above, the predominance of women among believers can be read through cultural frameworks. This situation is certainly linked with the importance of the concept of ancestors in the Taiwanese cultural environment. As has already been described the Catholic Church before the Second Vatican Council, did not allow the believers to have ancestors' shrine in their homes.

As a consequence, many of the old Catholic families which entered the Catholic Church before 1949 still do not have ancestors' shrine in their homes. When they have them, as in the Han people's religious world, the Catholics honored their ancestors at home, in the lineage hall, and in the church. They continue to participate in all the rites which were linked to their ancestors, such as Lunar New Year, Tomb Sweeping Day (*qing-*

---

7. Ma Ying-jeou (born 13 July 1950) is a Hong Kong-born Taiwanese politician who served as president of the Republic of China from 2008 to 2016. Previously, he served as justice minister from 1993 to 1996 and mayor of Taipei from 1998 to 2006. He served as chairman of the Kuomintang (KMT) from 2005 to 2007 and from 2009 to 2014.

8. Traditionally a woman was quite explicitly removed from the family of her birth (her *niangjia* 娘家) and affiliated to her husband's family (her *pojia* 婆家), a transition always very clearly symbolized in local marriage customs, despite their variation from one region to another. One of the first consequences of this particular situation is that it is easier for women to convert to Catholicism. In fact, it is a common opinion that they will anyway pray for ancestors belonging to a different lineage. Ahern also points out this fact when interviewing her informants: they told her that a daughter "does not belong to us. From birth on, girls are meant to belong to other people. They are supposed to die in other people's house" (Ahern, *The Cult of the Dead in a Chinese Village*, 127)

mingjie 清明節), Mid-Autumn Festival (*zhongqiujie* 中秋節), the celebration of death anniversaries, and so on.

The addition of a third place – the church – to the two where the reverence to ancestors are traditionally performed (The Freedman Domestic and Hall ceremonies), created new forms of veneration of ancestors. Communal celebrations are performed inside the church during the Chinese New Year and Tomb Sweeping Day. Apart from these traditional Chinese celebrations, the Catholic Church allows the performance of these rites also for the Catholic celebration of All Souls' Day. All Souls' Day is a Roman Catholic holiday celebrated on November 2nd (If that day falls on a Sunday, then All Souls' Day is moved to November 3rd since it is not permitted to wear black clothes on Sundays). Formally, it is known as *Commemoratio omnium Fidelium Defunctorum* or "Commemoration of all the Faithful Departed".

(a) Ancestors' Altar in the Resurrection Church

(b) Ancestors' Tablet of the Resurrection Church

Figure 2: Ancestors' Ceremonies in the Resurrection Church

During this month, in many of the churches of Taipei, an ancestors' shrine is placed inside the church beside the altar. The "Parish Ancestors' Tablet" (堂區祭祖靈位), two candles, the incense burner, flowers, and fruits are placed on this shrine (Fig. 2a).

After the Mass, the parish priest, helped by a parishioner, goes in front of the ancestors' shrine, offering incense, fruits, and flowers, sometimes fruits can be substituted by holy water. In the month of November, in the Resurrection church and also in the churches administrated by the CICM priests, pictures representing the departed friends and family members of parishioners (親友亡者) were hung on a panel in the back of the shrine (Fig. 2a). These communal celebrations were always officiated by the priest, but as the priest of the Resurrection church told me, the rites of Chinese New Year for the ancestors can be performed by one of the parishioners, male, and head of the family. Especially during the month of November, believers often ask the priest for a more specific mention of their own ancestors during the liturgy of the Mass. Before the beginning of the Mass, the believer went to the priest's office, wrote the name of the departed on a red envelope, and told the priest the reason behind this request for a particular mention. There are many reasons why people can ask for a special mention during the Mass. During the liturgy, the priest says the following prayer: "Remember, Lord, your people, especially those for whom we now pray (here the priest says the names of the departed for which the Mass is celebrated). Remember all of us gathered here before you."[9].

It is perhaps important to note that the dead are remembered within each mass, and those specific prayers for them are already present in the missal[10]. Here are some of them: "Remember, Lord, those who have died and have gone before us *marked with the sign of faith*, especially those for whom we now pray (at this point of the celebration the Priest mentions the names of the deceased or loved ones whom the celebrant or parishioner wishes to offer the Mass to before God). May these, and *all who sleep in Christ*, find in your presence light, happiness, and peace". Or "Remember our brothers and sisters who have gone to their rest in the hope of rising again; bring them and all the departed *into the light of your presence*". Or as follows: "Welcome into your kingdom our departed brothers and sisters, and all who have left this world *in your friendship*." Or again, "Remember those who have died *in the peace of Christ* and all the dead whose faith is known to you alone"[11]. But reading the same part of the liturgy translated in Chinese: "*Qiu ni ye chui nian suoyou de zuxian he qushi de ren, shi tamen xiang jian ni guanghui de sheng rong* 求你也垂念所有的祖先和去世的人,使他們享見你光輝的聖容"[12] it is possible to note that the concepts of "marked with the sign of faith", "left this world in your friendship" or "who have died in the peace of Christ" have disappeared from the text, extending the prayer to "all the departed". In a place where the believers are considered a minority and where most believers live in a completely non-Catholic environment (sometimes only one member of the family is converted to Catholicism), the symbolic boundaries of the peace of Christ must be widened to include the Taiwanese and non-baptized ancestors to whom prayers and Mass are dedicated.

To put this situation in relation to the concept of Universal Salvation preached by the Catholic Church. According to the Second Vatican Coun-

---

9. Roman Missal, "Eucharistic Prayers I–IV," in *Roman Missal*, Third Typical Edition (Vatican City: Congregation for Divine Worship / the Discipline of the Sacraments, 2001).
10. A missal is a liturgical book containing all instructions and texts necessary for the celebration of Mass throughout the year.
11. Missal, "Eucharistic Prayers I–IV," My emphasis.
12. Taiwan Bishops Conference, 主日感恩祭典*(甲)* (Taipei: 天主教教務協進會出版社, 1983).

cil[13], the ancestors are an integral part of the "Celestial Jerusalem" the "Triumphant Church" – the Church formed by the faithful who have already left this world – thus not just Catholic ancestors are embraced in this celestial family, but the document asserts that "all men" are "called to belong to the new people of God. Wherefore these people, while remaining one and only one, are to be spread throughout the whole world and must exist in all ages, so that the decree of God's will may be fulfilled. In the beginning, God made human nature one and decreed that all His children, scattered as they were, would finally be gathered together as one."[14]

This universal concept of salvation became evident inside the Mass liturgy, where the priest prays for all the ancestors and for all the dead. And, during the month of November, many churches that have ancestors' shrines simply display a generic phrase in order to remember all the dead, or if the ancestors' tablet is communal, a collective celebration is made for all the parishioners' ancestors. In my view, this concept illustrates that the Catholic Church is considered one, unique but large extended family, where all the believers are brothers and sisters who "received a spirit of adoption, through which we cry, Abba, Father!" (Rm. 8, 15). In this large family, "the Church" which further says "that Jerusalem which is above" (Galatians 4,26) is called "our mother". The Church is described as the spotless spouse of the spotless Lamb (Jesus), whom Christ "loved and for whom He delivered Himself up that He might sanctify her", whom He unites to Himself by an unbreakable covenant, and whom He unceasingly "nourishes and cherishes", and whom, once purified, "He willed to be cleansed and joined to Himself, subject to Him in love and fidelity, and whom, finally, He filled with heavenly gifts for all eternity, in order that we may know the love of God and of Christ for us, a love which surpasses all knowledge."[15].

I stressed these concepts because, in my view, this is one of the ways to understand the ancestors' rites in the Catholic world. If we make a simple comparison, we can see that while for believers of popular religions the rites have to be performed at home or at the ancestor hall, the Catholic believers add a third performing place, the church, which represents this new universal family, where all the members honor their own ancestors in order to venerate the ancestors of every believer, as well as the ancestor of each and every man: Jesus Christ. But "does God belong to Jews alone? Does he not belong to Gentiles, too? Yes, also to Gentiles" (Rom. 3,26). Therefore, all people are beneficiaries of God's love and mercy. Inside this new family, all the festivals dedicated to the *gui* (鬼 the Chinese ghosts) disappear, and they have no reasons to be celebrated. What disappears is what Feuchtwang defines as a spatial code: inside/outside, left/right, and

---

13. Lumen gentium, *Lumen gentium*, 1964, accessed March 8, 2022, https://www.vatican.va/archive/hist_councils/ii_vatican_council/documents/vat-ii_const_19641121_lumen-gentium_en.html.
14. Lumen gentium, see also Jn. 11, 52.
15. Lumen gentium.

4.2 The Taiwanese Catholic Ancestors' Rites

upper/lower[16]. All the rites are directed toward the inside, in the church as in the home. No rites are performed toward the outside (the rituals that are usually performed to the Gods and to the ghosts).

According to Feuchtwang[17], this spatial code is a way to differentiate soldiers, notably, gods or gods of heaven, and also to distinguish Gods and *gui*. In conjunction with the spatial code, there are other means of making distinctions in the presentation of offerings: through an ordered sequence of offerings of food. This "order of privilege" represents a syntagmatic hierarchical order. But this order suffers radical changes inside the Church's rites: all the ancestors have been honored the same way in the funerals, with incense, fruits, and flowers (and in some churches also with wine and holy water). No food is offered to God, just incense and sometimes flowers (which are especially offered to the Blessed Virgin Mary).

In summary, it is possible to see that both spatially and hierarchically, one of the categories disappeared: the category of *gui*.

What I have explained above is, in my view, the fundamental approach of the Taiwanese Catholic Church toward what we call the Taiwanese popular religion. A semantic change of some symbols of the faith in order to provide the native people with a new key for the interpretation of – in some ways dominant – religious concepts. But, according to what I wrote above, how can it be explained that many believers still believe and are scared of ghosts that they still continue to see? How can it be explained that many believers still burn paper money at their ancestors' graves or that others go to the temple during the Spring Festival? How can we explain the fact that many believers participate in the Mass only when they encounter some problems, or when they don't participate in Church activities at all? Why is there a great emphasis on the miracle-working experience of the faith?

It is evident that there are no easy answers, but what I want to try to do, and what I want to demonstrate is that these questions can be answered only by putting them into a single cultural framework. I believe religion with its sacred symbols is embodied in a wider symbolic system which is commonly called culture. As I will illustrate in the next chapter, Catholic believers of Taiwan are still linked in a deep way with the traditional symbolic system, which means that the Catholics use symbols from both religious and cultural systems in order to face and solve daily problems.

---

16. Feuchtwang, "Domestic and communal worship in Taiwan."
17. Feuchtwang.

Chapter 5

Cultural Interpretations

The complex encounter between two cultures is not understandable only in terms of the analysis and comparisons of their respective cosmologies. Cosmology, using an expression of Durkheim, is a "Collective Representation". In Durkheim's view, Sacred Collective representations help in the process to order and make sense of the world, and they can also express and interpret social relationships. the sacred is created through rituals, and what is deemed sacred is what morally binds individuals to society. This moral bond then becomes a cognitive bond that shapes the categories we use to understand the social world[1]. These collective mental representations offer a coherent explanation of the origin, evolution, and eventual fate of the universe from a religious perspective. Nevertheless, they are embedded within a larger symbolic system called culture. Within a specific culture, religion with its cosmology and sacred symbols plays a very important role. At least, in Taiwan, is possible to assert that the conception of the world made by the complex cosmology, which underlies the practices of popular religion, it is in some ways regarded as the dominant symbolic power. This is very important because the influence of this cosmology is felt in many aspects of the everyday life of people.

Among the rites for the ancestors, the symbolic meaning of the tablets of the ancestors, take up an important part. In fact, within the tablets resides one of the ancestor's souls, for this reason, the tablets are never moved and people are careful not to touch them so as not to irritate the ancestor. Furthermore, behind the tablet, very often the genealogy of the family is listed. By putting the ancestor tablet on the altar, people symbolically unify the ancestors and honor the family lineage. Incense is lit before the altar daily, significant announcements are made before them, and offerings

---

1. Emile Durkheim, *Les formes élémentaires de la vie religieuse. Le système totémique en Australie* [in Français], 1968, cinquième édition (Paris: Les Presses Universitaires de France, 1912), 19, accessed March 8, 2022, http://classiques.uqac.ca/classiques/Durkheim_emile/formes_vie_religieuse/formes_vie_religieuse.html.

such as favorite foods, beverages, and spirit money are given bi-monthly and on special occasions, such as Qingming Festival and Zhong Yuan Festival. Many people believe that ancestors exist as supernatural spirits and these spirits would respond to secular requests from worship[2]. Since the soul of the deceased is believed to dwell in the ancestor tablet, this makes the tablets an important symbol. If it is possible to consider ancestor worship and all related practices as a religious system[3], I believe it is possible to consider the tablets of the ancestors as important sacred symbols. As Geertz pointed out[4], the function of sacred symbols is to synthesize the ethos of people; these symbols certainly have the ability to mold the worldview of people, introducing the believer to a type of specific sets of dispositions. I would say that the dispositions created by these sacred symbols coexist with other dispositions dictated by practical activities linked to the social environment, the political system, the financial situation, and (last but not least in Taiwan) the effect of the so-called process of globalization.

5.1 The same service to the dead as to the living 事死如事生

Inside the complex and – at least for those in the West – very different conceptions of the world, man and spirits (ancestors, ghosts, or deities) physically share the same living space, the same living time, and share the same human preoccupations or bodily needs. As Francis Hsu noted in his Under the Ancestors' Shadow, "the attitude of the living toward the dead and that of the living are functionally one. The relationship of the living with the dead is essentially modeled upon that of the living with the living. In glorifying the dead, it is both idealized and it sets the standard and pattern for kinship relationship."[5]

As we saw above, there is a Chinese proverb that says, "The same service to the dead as to the living; to the absent as to the present" (*shisi ru shisheng* 事死如事生). In some ways, the necessities of ancestors' worship give parents an additional imperative to have sons in order to perform the rites and thus secure eternal life for their parents and grandparents. "There are three things which are unfilial," says Mencius, "and to have no posterity is the greatest of them" (*Buxiao yousan,wuhou weida* 不孝有三，無後為大)[6]. Thus, we can say that all those who already left, who presently live in, and who will in the future live in this world all share the same

---

2. Anning Hu, "Ancestor Worship in Contemporary China: An Empirical Investigation," Publisher: The Chinese University of Hong Kong Press, *China Review* 16, no. 1 (2016): 173.
3. Batairwa, *Meaning and Controversy within Chinese Ancestor Religion*.
4. Geertz, "The interpretation of cultures."
5. Hsu, *Under the Ancestors' Shadow*, 245.
6. James Legge, *The works of Mencius* [in Chinese and English] (New York: Dover Publications, 1970).

5.1 The same service to the dead as to the living 事死如事生

lifetime and the same existential world. In other words, all these categories live in one eternal present. Because of the complex interrelations between these categories, the bounds between the people who are living and those who have died (whatever kind of being they have become: an ancestor, a ghost or a divinity) are very strong and real for Taiwanese people. One of the consequences of this situation is that in the Taiwanese world, to talk exclusively in terms of "natural" and "supernatural", as we are used to in Western terms, it is at least reductive. As I mentioned in previous chapters (see chapter 2), I believe that culture cannot be considered as a structure, I prefer to consider it as a public system of meanings embodied in symbols, symbols that share dynamic and creative relationships. Religious symbols are embodied in these symbolic systems, and share these attributes.

By directly analyzing religious symbols, it is possible to try to understand how some Taiwanese Catholics still use symbolic values originating from the popular religion to interpret the Catholic religion, and how these symbols are re-used and "re-semantized" by the Catholic believers and priests.

The study of the reverence for ancestors' phenomenon brings us to understand how Taiwanese people consider the world of the afterlife. As I mentioned in Chapter 2, anthropologists commonly make a clear distinction between three classes of supernatural beings: gods, ancestors, and ghosts. These studies often put these entities in relationship with the bureaucratic structures of the former Chinese empire[7] where the gods are metaphorically representing the imperial bureaucrats, the ancestors represent important local characters, and where the ghosts, according to the society's change[8], are considered as brigands or beggars. Yet, according to my experience in Taiwan, there could be a more basic way to define and divide these three categories of supernatural beings. Firstly, the dead who are worshiped by their own descendants are considered ancestors. Secondly, those who do not have descendants to worship them will become ghosts. Lastly, the dead who are worshiped by a multitude of people, not only by their own families, are considered gods. I personally believe that this somewhat simple division could represent a point of view that Taiwanese people share in order to define supernatural beings. Thus, as far as Taiwanese Catholic people are concerned, this kind of division is still present and especially meaningful.

The relationships between supernatural beings and those who are still living are, for many Taiwanese people, physical and direct. The dead and the living share the same time and the same living space and, perhaps most importantly, the same bodily needs.

In order to introduce how the concept of the afterlife depicted by the Taiwanese traditional culture influences the vision and the actions of some

---

7. Wolf, "Gods, ghosts, and ancestors"; Ahern, *Chinese ritual and politics.*; Feuchtwang, "Domestic and communal worship in Taiwan"; Feuchtwang, *The Imperial Metaphor*.
8. Weller, *Unities and Diversities in Chinese Religion*.

Catholic believers, I am going, to introduce and analyze some concrete examples that I encountered during my fieldwork. I will keep the traditional Taiwanese after-world categories of gods, ancestors, and ghosts as a guideline to the reader, to make them understand how this structure still influences the religious approach of many of Catholic faithful I interviewed.

However, before introducing these categories and the material I collected, I believe it is necessary to introduce first some of the main concepts that form the cosmology of the Taiwanese popular religion.

5.2 The Concept of Time

The concept of time is particularly important because the two different ways to conceive religious phenomena offered by Catholicism and by the Taiwanese traditional popular beliefs encompass two different conceptions of time. For believers of popular religion, in contrast to Catholics, there are not many fixed or cyclical dates on which a believer must go to the temple in the current year. Usually, people go to the temple in order to solve specific needs related to bad luck, illness, school exams, and so on. This is probably related to another concept, the concept of *Ling* (靈), which I will present in the following pages.

There are certainly some dates, during the year when Popular Religion practitioners go to the temple such as during lunar new year celebrations, or during ghost offerings on the fifteenth day of the eighth month of the lunar calendar (The Ghost Festival, also known as the *Zhongyuan* Festival 中元節), But there is no regular or weekly celebration like Mass. In the following section, both the lunar calendar (Chinese traditional calendar) and the Gregorian calendar (Western traditional calendar) will be mentioned, the latter being particularly relevant in defining the relationship with the liturgical calendar (the Catholic Church's way to look at the time).

5.2.1 Lunar Calendar

The Chinese calendar is based on Chinese astrology, due to the close connection between Geomancy, horoscope, Astrology and Astronomy, and the difficulty in determining exactly where one begins and the other ends. The Yin and Yang, and the five elements, together with the eight diagrams *bagua* (八卦), enter largely into Chinese astrological calculation. In the calculation of a fortunate time to undertake any given enterprise, a favorable combination of eight horoscope characters is identified. These eight characters are the four pairs of characters representing the year, month, day, and hour. The characters denoting the year are those of the Twelve Branches (*shierdizhi* 十二地支) and Celestial Stems (*shitiangan* 十天干) in the Chinese cycle (Cycle of sixty *huajiazi* 花甲子). Those denoting the month are the combination of Branches and Stems assigned to that month (*yuejinquanbei* 月令全備), referring to the epoch in the annual cycle. Those denoting the day are the combinations of Branches and Stems assigned in the lunar calendar to that day, referring to the epoch in the lunar monthly cycle. Those denoting the hour are the combination of Branches and Stems representing that hour, referring to the epoch in the daily solar cycle.

By considering the mutual affinities of these eight characters as referred to as the Yin and Yang, Five elements, etc., the good or bad auspices of any undertaking may be determined. The same system applies to birth, death, marriage, and in fortune-telling. The eighty cyclical characters (*bazi* 八字), pertaining to the time of the birth, are communicated between betrothed persons and occasionally between intimate friends or sworn brothers.

Chinese calendars consist of full directions as to omens and portents, and what undertakings can best be carried out on each particular day, all worked out by the rules of Astrology. This is very important because in practice these things can inhibit a marriage between two people, anticipate or delay the birth of a child, etc. It seems, as Geertz wrote, that with this kind of calendar "they don't tell you what time it is; they tell you what kind of time it is"[9]. This phenomenon, in my opinion, is critical. As we saw above, there are only a few occasions when it is crucial to go to the temple in the year, probably only during the Chinese New Year or on the occasion of a particular god's "birthday". Otherwise, people go to the temple when they feel a specific need (bad luck, exams, etc.). As we saw above, according to this behavior – in a the Western view – the conception of time and the common conception of religion are just matters of practicality; there is nothing transcendental or mystical in these representations.

The result is that a person will often go to the temple when the need for divine intervention is greater. The frequency of visits will decrease when everyday life goes on without hitches or particular problems.

5.2.2 Gregorian Solar Calendar and Liturgical Time

The concept of the Gregorian Solar calendar refers to the Western way to calculate and measure time. In Taiwan, as almost everywhere else in the world, this way designates the daily schedule (time to wake up, to work, to have lunch, to go back home, etc.). Other than this, it provides a weekly concept of time: from Monday to Friday (or more often until Saturday), one has to work, while the weekend – or sometimes Sunday only – is time for rest and relaxation. In this regard, Taiwan follows this international standard. This vision of time is embodied already a liturgical meaning: it is the Church's concept of time. "By the seventh day God had finished the work he had been doing; so on the seventh day, he rested from all his work. And God blessed the seventh day and made it holy because on it he rested from all the work of creating that he had done." (Genesis 2). God worked for six days and on the seventh day, he took a rest. Just like a common

---
9. Geertz, "The interpretation of cultures," 393.

5 Cultural Interpretations

worker. This vision is at the base of the modern, Western conception of time. Why do I consider this to be so important? Because the liturgical time stretches on a full year, with the same specific and recurrent festivities – Christmas, Easter, etc. However, there is another shorter cycle of time, which stretches over a week, and which culminates at the Sunday Mass.

Here, Pierre Bourdieu's concepts of "habitus", and the other concept of "practical activities", allows comprehension and to account for the importance of this Catholic conception of time[10]. In Bourdieu's view, ritual practices such as "invocations" originate from some collective torments. Invocations are expressed in a collective language, like music. Therefore, in these practices are embodied all the intentions, hopes, and requests expressed by symbolic words and symbolic gestures. Words and gestures, which realized the meaning of the world without changing it. To this definition of ritual practices, try to link Bourdieu's concept of "habitus", which is the key in order to understanding "cultural reproduction". The habitus is able to generate regular ways of conduct, which can influence social life. In this way, ritual practices can be seen as a habitus, a regular way to express symbolic words and gestures that give meaning to the world without changing it. It is therefore through the performance of daily or constant practices linked to these invocations that the habitus of the faithful is created and preserved, and it is through this habitus that the faithful give "new" - Catholics - meaning to the experiences of his life. As Richard Madsen argues, today Chinese folk-Catholicism shows similar characteristics to folk-Buddhism. "For most rural Catholics, most of the time, the faith is completely melted with the structures of family and village life. One becomes a Catholic by being born in a Catholic family in a Catholic village, not by making any faith commitment to a doctrine of universal salvation. Such Catholics seem indistinguishable in terms of mentality, morality, and lifestyle from non-Christian villagers, the only major difference being the performance of different rituals to mark important events in the life cycle"[11], and again, "Many complicated ties do connect village-level Catholic communities throughout China with one another and with the universal Catholic Church. First, local communities all share a common, distinctive time framework. They celebrate festivals according to a common liturgical calendar"[12]. According to this analysis, it can be asserted that the faith of the believers expresses itself through some habits, the sharing of a common experience of time, as well as a common calendar.

As above-mentioned, the most important and representative rite in the Catholic Church is the celebration of the Mass. Generally, in Taipei city,

---

10. Bourdieu, *Raisons pratiques*.
11. Richard Madsen, "Catholicism as Chinese Folk Religion," in *China and Christianity: Burdened Past, Hopeful Future: Burdened Past, Hopeful Future*, ed. Stephen Uhalley and Xiaoxin Wu (New York: Routledge, 2001), 73.
12. Richard Madsen, *China's Catholics: Tragedy and Hope in an Emerging Civil Society* [in en] (University of California Press, 1998), ISBN: 9780520213265.

almost all the parishes perform this type of celebration every day, but the most important one is of course the Mass that takes place on Sunday. This Mass is the one in which everyone of the faithful should participate.

It is first necessary to introduce a particular custom that is quite common in every Catholic church all over the world. Every believer can offer a Mass in order to pray for his own needs or for his ancestors; this means that within the rite of the Mass the priest will pray specifically for the needs of the believer who offered the Mass. Usually, the believer gives a free donation of money. In the Resurrection church, a red envelope containing a certain amount of money is given – before the beginning of the Mass – to the priest. The particular prayer's request or the name of the ancestor is written on the envelope.

In the Resurrection church, the Mass was celebrated only on Sunday, but some believers went every day to the nearby St. Teresa church, a church built by the C.I.C.M. Missionaries, which in that period was administered by the same parish priest, Father Martin. Going every day to the church, I had the opportunity to meet several parishioners who attended the Mass only once over a period of two or three years. Every visit was linked to urgent needs: a request for healing for a sick person, help with their child's university entrance examination, requests to ease the tense ties within a family, and many other needs.

Mister Lin was a sixty-year-old parishioner. In more than four years, I met him only three times. He was the owner of a noodles market stand near Longshan night market, one of the most famous in Taipei. The first time I met him was during the SARS (Severe Acute Respiratory Syndrome) crisis, the respiratory disease that spread in some Asian countries, between November 2002 and July 2003. At that time, he was understandably in trouble because of that disease (as most of the population in the old district of Wanhua) because the night market was closed for a long time. He offered the Mass asking for the end of the disease. After the disease ceased, I went several times to the night market. I naturally met him there, and he told me that he was not going to Mass because he was very busy. I did not meet Mister Lin at the church again until four years later. At that time, his wife was in the hospital because of heart surgery, in this case, he came to the Sunday Mass in order to offer a Mass for his wife's health, and pray for a good outcome of the surgery and her entire stay at the hospital. After the surgery, he returned one more time to the church to offer another mass in order to thank God for the fast recovery of his wife from the surgery.

Another case is about an old woman who was very worried about her son. She did not frequently attend the Mass, but on some occasions, she came to the St. Teresa church in order to offer a Mass for her son. The other parishioners told me about her family problems. Nevertheless, not only old people behave this way toward church activities.

The case of a particular young person is very interesting. The individual in question received his undergraduate degree and went to the Church to

5 Cultural Interpretations

express his gratitude to God, and at the same time to ask His help for his forth-coming military service. He offered the Mass for two consecutive Sundays. Despite the fact that he lived very near to the church and he was studying in Taipei, those were the only two times I saw him at the Mass.

Sometimes believers I had never seen before came to the church and offered a Mass for their ancestors, sometimes on the occasion of a death anniversary, but sometimes only to pray for them, to wish them peace and eternal life. However, the range of motives for these offerings includes requests to find a job, God's help because the pressure at work was too much, or generic prayers for their health (*shentijiankan* 身體健康).

Most of the examples I cited above concern people who came to the church only to offer a Mass in order to solve their problems. These situations represent a clear contrast that arises from the different ways to understand and live the Chinese cultural conception of time. This conception of course bases itself on principles of Cosmology, and especially on the practical way to experience the religious construction of time of this Cosmology. These believers live their faith as their neighbors do or as their schoolmates do: by going to church only when they feel particular needs or to thank God for an unexpected fortune. By living within an environment of popular religion, Catholics, after their baptism, will still maintain their previous patterns of conduct. Those who have been baptized at an early childhood age tend to follow the common social pattern of conduct toward religious behavior. And Because they are not involved in practical activities like the Holy Mass, it becomes very hard for these people to understand and be involved in Catholic Cosmology.

In this way, it is possible to understand the effort that the Catholic Church put into the teaching of practical concepts like the daily prayer of the Holy Rosary, which allows believers to meditate weekly on the mystery of the birth of Jesus, his death, and resurrection. In the same way, it is possible to understand why the week of Catholic people is structured to emphasize the weekend: on Friday – traditionally considered as the day on which Jesus died – believers are advised not to eat meat as a form of penitence, and on Sunday all the Church celebrates the resurrection of Christ. The hope is that these everyday practices would bring believers to model their lifestyle – and their daily activities – on the Catholic Cosmological structures.

5.3 The Concept of *Ling* 靈

As we noted above, one of the fundamental concepts that regulate the relationships between the various deities and the worshipers is the concept of Ling. The choice of a deity and of a temple are generally made to match the function of the deity to some specific need: if this god satisfies my urgent situations or helps me solve my problems, I will continue to go to him, and otherwise, I will change deity and temple. Here are some examples of how this conception can influence the conduct of Catholic people.

During the time of my fieldwork, I participated in a Bible study group. Generally, this kind of study group is composed of believers who want to study in depth the Holy Bible with the help of a priest or a nun, and with the aim to increase their knowledge of Sacred Scriptures.

In this Bible study group, I met Mrs. Chen. She was a fifty-year-old married woman who lived in Taipei. She was baptized and continued to attend the Mass or the other activities of the Church. She told me that she was the only person in her family who believed in Jesus, her husband and her child was involved in the practices of popular religion. Mrs. Chen told me a very interesting story about her son. As is common among the young Taiwanese, he went to consult the temple's fortuneteller, the *Suanming* 算命 to ask some questions about his studies. After the fortune-teller responded, he asked something about his mother. But at this point the fortune-teller said that his mother already belonged to Jesus, so he did not have any power over her. When the son came home, he immediately told his mother: "your Jesus is really strong!" (*ni yesu zhen lihai* 你耶穌真厲害). Surprised by this statement Mrs. Chen questioned her son, and discovered what the fortune-teller previously told her son. Commenting on this fact, Mrs. Chen said that she was already sure that Jesus is stronger because He is more Ling, which means He really answers her prayers.

A nun once told me that she had witnessed an interesting episode. She was working in a Catholic store near Taipei's main station, selling books and religious objects. Once a young man and his mother came inside the store looking for some sacred images. While examining different objects, the young boy asked the nun which object was the most powerful (*shenme dongxi bijiao ling* 什麼東西比較靈?). This kind of term is not used among Catholics but is very common among the believers of the Taiwanese popular religion. Curious, the nun asked the cause of this question, and the boy answered that some nights before he dreamed of his grandmother who passed away not long ago. The grandmother told the nephew in dreams that in the place where she now was, there was no Buddha or Guanyin, but there was only a man on the cross. So, the grandmother has recommended the nephew forget all the popular religious practices and look for that particular symbol: a man on the cross.

Li Chonghao is a young man who joined the guitar activity group of the Resurrection church. Every Sunday he and two or three other youths played the guitar during the Sunday Mass. He told me that his grandmother (all of his family members were Catholics) told him that for any problems he had to go to the Holy Rosary church because the Blessed Virgin Mary of the Holy Rosary church was very ling. He felt this was very strange because, as he asked me, "isn't the Blessed Virgin Mary the same in every part of the world? Why must I go to the Holy Rosary church to pray the Blessed Virgin Mary?" The Holy Rosary church is another church administrated by the C.I.C.M. Congregation, and it is located in the Wanhua district. The Holy Rosary church is the biggest church in the Wanhua district, and many people attend the Sunday Mass there.

In the same district of Wanhua is the above-mentioned St. Teresa Church. St. Teresa was nominated by the Pope as the patron saint of Taiwan, and one of the first Sanctuaries dedicated to Saint Teresa in Taiwan was the Church in Wanhua (小德蘭朝聖地). For this reason, on the annual celebration of Saint Teresa, many Catholics come from all over Taiwan in order to honor this saint. The celebrations stretch over a full week and the priest told me that in that week there are believers who make an offer of over 80,000 new Taiwanese dollars and this is for each day of the celebration[13]. The priest told me that the first time he saw such a significant donation, he could not believe it. However, as a believer explained to me, such a phenomenon happens because people think that this saint is very Ling. This is one of the reasons why many Taiwanese Catholic women choose the name Teresa when they are baptized.

Another phenomenon that in my view originates from this concept of ling is the fact that particularly after their baptism – especially if the baptism is received at the adult age – people are inclined to have many questions about their new faith and about the right way to practice and experience it. Questions often concern theological and intellectual doubts, practical problems that arise because of the contrast between the new faith and their "old" lifestyle, issues related to life in the family or at their workplace, at school, and so on. A priest once told me that people, especially if freshly baptized, often ask many questions, and if the priest's answers do not completely satisfy them, believers will go to consult another priest until they find answers that satisfy them. In my view, this is a type of custom that derives from the fact that believers, even though they are already baptized, still use the cultural system within which they were born, but adapt it to their new condition of Catholics.

5.3.1 Chinese *Ling* and Christian Miracles

This concept of supernatural power, Ling, is in some ways linked to the Catholic concept of miracles. In the case of miracles, the believers, just as with the concept of Ling, ask the help of God – but in the Catholic tradition the help of the Blessed Virgin Mary and other saints – to solve a difficulty which appears humanly unsolvable. In this case, after the successful resolution of the initial problem, the believer's faith is consolidated and gets stronger. In fact, these types of miracle-working events have implications not only for the Catholic religion but for the so-called Taiwanese New Religion; Jochim in his article about the study of the religion of the Yellow Emperor (*Xuanyuanjiao* 軒轅教) stresses that a cult of healing developed within the religion as a result of certain healing "miracles" in the

---

13. Approximately 2400 euros.

early 1970s[14]. As the author points out, the involvement of religion in the most famous cases of "miracle" was almost accidental. The case is that of an elderly man named Luo A-fu, who had a stroke that left him half-paralyzed. A devoted grandson found a flyer being distributed by religious people in the area, burned it, and put the ashes in the tea for his grandfather to drink.

When Luo Afu began to recover, his grandson attributed this to the efficacy of the Yellow Emperor and frequently took his grandfather to the Taipei Holy Palace of the Yellow Emperor to worship and drink "sacred water" (*jingcha* 敬茶, "tea offered in respect [and blessed by the Yellow Emperor]"). The result, in their minds, was the complete recovery of Luo A-fu, followed by his years of service to the temple as a volunteer helper. News of this event was largely responsible for mass conversions (of reportedly more than 1,000 people) that subsequently occurred in Guandu (關渡) and Danshui (淡水)[15]. Although in the doctrinal writing of the founder of the religion Wang Hansheng (王寒生) there is no special mention of faith healing, even for him it has become an accepted dimension of the religion[16]. In this case, it seems to me that Taiwanese people use their own cosmology, which is part of a specific cultural context, to understand and interpret this new religion, using in this particular case the concept of ling, and this even though the founder himself did not stress it before the Luo A-fu miracle.

According to Lozada, Catholic, and non-Catholic Chinese villagers attribute similar kinds of good luck and unusual experiences to the supernatural. Catholics attribute them to God, non-Catholics to ancestors, or perhaps to Bodhisattva[17].

Similarly, the fact that many believers I interviewed started to explain their experience of faith by telling me about an episode that according to them is indubitably a miracle and more important proof of the truthful nature of their religion.

Mister Gao was a seventy-year-old man. He had been converted at the age of eighteen, while his wife came from a traditional Catholic family. One of his daughters became a nun, another daughter was a very active parishioner at the Resurrection church. He liked to talk to me about miracles because he felt these were real facts of significant importance. Yet for him, the priest sometimes did not pay enough attention to these experiences.

Mister Gao told me about a lot of miracles that occurred to some old parishioners. One of them concerned an old woman who was a farmer. She was very poor, and one day she bought a bag of fertilizer, only one because she did not have more money. On the way home, the weather started to change and she distinctly heard the sound of the rain behind her. She

---

14. Christian Jochim, "Flowers, Fruit, and Incense Only: Elite versus Popular in Taiwan's Religion of the Yellow Emperor," *Modern China* 16, no. 1 (January 1990): 14.
15. Zhou, Yonglan 周用蘭, "從社會人類學的觀點看臺灣一個新興宗教：軒轅教" (國立台灣大學考古人類學系學士論文, National Taiwan University, 1972), 27–30.
16. Jochim, "Flowers, Fruit, and Incense Only," 15.
17. Eriberto P. Lozada, *God Aboveground: Catholic Church, Postsocialist State, and Transnational Processes in a Chinese Village* (Stanford University Press, 2001), 95.

5 Cultural Interpretations

started to pray to the Blessed Virgin Mary because that bag of fertilizer was the only one that she could buy, and if the fertilizer would get wet, it would start dissolving and she would lose her money and all capacity to fertilize her field. She started to run as fast as she could, continuously hearing the sound of the rain and at the same time reciting the Holy Rosary. When she arrived near the village, she met a young man, and with his help reached home without being caught by the rain. Once at home, she discovered that the rain was following her all the time, but it inexplicably did not catch her. The old woman explained this fact as a miracle made by the Blessed Virgin Mary who she had prayed continuously on her way home.

Another miracle told to me by Mister Gao was also related to a poor woman. She bought a cabbage, but because it was treated with poisonous chemicals when the family members ate it, all of them got sick and a son who died. The only person who did not have any kind of problem was that woman, even though she had eaten that poisonous cabbage. She was persuaded that the cause of this was the direct intervention of God because she was the only Catholic in the family.

As Mister Gao told me, the priest did not pay too much attention to these stories, because he maintained that the faith of believers cannot depend only on miracles or on divine manifestations.

According to Madsen, believers consider God as the author of these miracles, usually through the intercession of the Blessed Virgin Mary, and this without asking the opinion of a priest or following any ecclesiastical rule[18]. In agreement with what Madsen argued above, Lozada sustains that God grants these miracles, usually through the intercession of the Virgin Mary, without going through any priest or following any ecclesiastical rule. The only necessary condition is that the individual believer sincerely seeks God's help. The miracles are independent of any human effort. Sometimes, miracles manifest themselves in the form of a direct call by God to serve the Church, without the believers needing the approval of official Catholic Church authority[19]. Nevertheless, for most believers, these extraordinary experiences confirm and strengthen their faith.

---

18. Madsen, *China's Catholics*, 94.
19. Lozada, *God Aboveground*, 94.

Chapter 6

Gods, Ghosts, and the Ancestors

6.1 Gods

It is almost impossible for Western people who come to Taipei not to be surprised by the impressive number of temples and representations of divinities that are present in this city. The divinities worshiped in these temples are generally historical characters who may have helped people in trouble, like Tudigong (土地公) or Mazu (媽祖). They can be mythological figures, such as the Jade Emperor, Yuhuangdadi (玉皇大帝), the first farmer (神農), or the God of War (關帝), etc. There are a considerable number of temples, and consequently, a significant number of deities that are able to answer the most particular needs of people. In addition to the more common temples like that of Tudigong, who is considered the guardian of the territory on which his temples are built, or Mazu called Queen of Heaven (*tianhou* 天后) or Queen of Heaven and Holy Mother (*tianshangshengmu* 天上聖母), there are many deities which can be prayed to. Before school examination, students usually pray to the God of Culture (*wenchan* 文昌) or Confucius (孔子). When a woman is pregnant, she would pray to the Goddess of Childbirth (註生娘娘), or refer herself to the Pond Point Madam, the goddess who controls the pool of blood, the dead, ghosts, and pregnancy. Farmers refer themselves to the God of Agriculture (*shennong* 神農), to Tudigong, and so on.

These temples are open to all people, without any distinction of sex, age, status, or nationality. It is important to observe, that temple worshipers cannot be considered parishioners in the Western sense. In fact, there are no records of temple worshipers, and more importantly, if the wishes or the prayers of the worshipers go unanswered, it is considered legitimate for the worshiper to abandon the god or gods in question and to seek help from different ones[1].

Usually, religious ceremonies in folk temples are simple, pragmatic, personal, and in most cases conducted without the intervention of either a Taoist or a Buddhist priest. Especially in the big temples of Taipei city, like Longshan temple (龍山寺), Baoangong (保安宮), or Xintiangong (行天宮), people are used to worshipping the main gods as Guanyin (觀音) and Tiangong (天公), and then go to the god (or gods) of their choice. After praying silently, the worshiper may move on to the other gods of the temple and repeat this procedure[2]. This kind of prayer can be considered a common practice for most Taiwanese people. It is not uncommon, inside the school, to meet students who want go to worship (*wo yao qu baibai* 我要去拜拜) a particular divinity because of a coming examination, because of sentimental troubles with their loved one, and so on.

At this point, a question may be asked: if these deities are present in more than one temple, why do people prefer to go to Longshan temple even if it may be more distant from their home? To answer this, consider an additional element: the god or gods worshiped by people are always believed to have Ling (靈), therefore, to be efficacious and effective for the individual worshiper[3]. The success of temples such as the Baoangong or the Longshan temple is attributed to the proven Ling of their gods and goddesses. There is a sentence I heard several times: it is not important for a temple to be big, what matters is that the deity is Ling.

6.1.1 The Blessed Virgin Mary

In addition to the considerations above, a particular place in this discussion of Gods must be reserved for the Blessed Virgin Mary. Woman deities are already present in the rich Chinese pantheon. The more important and maybe the more worshiped is Guanyin. The most usual and popular representation of this Goddess is a beautiful and gracious woman, who holds a child in her arms and wears a rosary around her neck. This iconography has been reused in order to paint the image of the Blessed Virgin Mary; at the point where it is hard sometimes to distinguish between the two figures (Figures 3a and 3b). My point is not that Catholic people consider the Blessed Virgin Mary as the Christian reference of Guanyin, but I want to stress that, when honoring the "new" supernatural figure, Taiwanese Catholics still maintain the forms they learned through their involvement in popular religious practices from an early age, which are linked to the cultural system they inhabit.

---

1. David K. Jordan, *Gods, ghosts, and ancestors: the folk religion of a Taiwanese village* (Berkeley: University of California Press, 1972), 103.
2. Eleanor B. Morris Wu, *From China to Taiwan. Historical, Anthropological, and Religious Perspectives* (Monumenta Serica Institute, 2004).
3. Jordan, *Gods, ghosts, and ancestors*, 103.

According to Lozada, the Virgin Mary, as a source of charismatic authority, has commanded more widespread devotion in different cultures than any other Roman Catholic saint has[4]. The blessed Virgin Mary, like Guanyin, serves as a bridge between the mundane needs and hopes of human beings and the strength and majesty of transcendental spiritual power. In his discussion about the Blessed Virgin Mary, Lozada particularly stresses how devotees have revered her largely through relics, shrines, and apparitions: because in her ascension to Heaven, the Blessed Virgin Mary left no body to venerate or location, like a tomb or a shrine where to venerate the place of her assumption. On the other hand, She appeared in many forms which vary locally. Indeed, the Blessed Virgin Mary is unique in both her universality and her particularity[5].

(a) The Blessed Virgin Mary (b) Guanyin

Figure 3: The Blessed Virgin Mary (a) and Guanyin (b), painted in traditional Chinese dress and holding a baby

According to Madsen Mary is primarily the one who helps us in our trials, defends us from our enemies, heals us when we are sick, and keeps us from sin. The eager acceptance of the reverence of Mary by Chinese Catholics was due at least partly to Mary's similarity to Buddhist Guanyin and to the Eternal Mother of Northern Chinese secret societies[6].

---

4. Lozada, *God Aboveground*, 34.
5. Lozada, 34.
6. Madsen, *China's Catholics*, 88.

The Blessed Virgin Mary appeared in Taiwan, on the Shenmu Shanzhuang Mountain (聖母山莊) in the County of Yilan. Every year the parishioners of the Resurrection church go there for a pilgrimage. I am in full agreement with Madsen (1998:94) who argues that the apparitions of Mary are deeply connected with the general belief in miracles of Chinese people[7].

Lozada further points out that the belief of Chinese Catholics in apparitions of Mary are closely connected to their general belief in miracles, a belief that defies all the education they received at school upon secular science. Catholics talk a lot about miracles.

In his work, Lozada argues that almost all the Catholics he asked said they had personally experienced miracles, and they often claimed that their faith was strong precisely because they had been blessed with such experiences. The most commonly cited miracles are humble acts of unexplained good fortune[8], such as the miracles told to me by Mister Gao.

However, what I want to stress now is how the iconographic assimilation of the image of the Blessed Virgin Mary with Guanyin or with Mazu – also called Holy Mother (*shengmu* 聖母) – aligns with the assimilation of the symbolic behavior of believers toward these figures.

Such behavior implies a series of bows in front of the statue, and also the possibility to worship her by offering flowers instead of incense. A young man, who was the only one in his family to believe in God, told me that when he brought his mother to the church, the first thing that she mother did was to go in front of the statue of the Blessed Virgin Mary and bow repeatedly, after which she told him that she was very surprised that Mazu was in churches. This last example could help us to understand how the Chinese iconography of the Blessed Virgin Mary is interpreted on the basis of cultural images that people already know, images deeply linked to a specific cultural system.

6.2 Ancestors

As previously discussed there are relationships between the reverence for ancestors and the Confucian concept of filial piety, which, according to the teachings of the great philosopher, consists of obedience, serving one's parents throughout life according to the propriety (li 禮), burying them according to the propriety, and in sacrificing to them according to the propriety[9].

The great and deep meaning that relates the concept of filial piety with the ancestors' rites, endorsed Ricci's decision to allow these kinds of rites, but the relationship between living people and ancestors is true in another

---

7. Madsen, *China's Catholics*, 94.
8. Lozada, *God Aboveground*, 94.
9. James Legge, *Confucian analects: The great learning, and the doctrine of the mean* (New York: Dover Publications, 1971), Bk. iii., pt. i., c. v., v. 4.

way. A common Chinese sentence describes the ancestors as the gods of the home (*zuxian shi jiali de shen* 祖先是家裡的神).

I was in Taipei when, after a big road accident occurred in the southern part of Taiwan, local news transmitted images of Buddhist monks and Taoist priests who were moving around the crash site in order to find souls of the deceased and guide them to their ancestors' tablets (招魂).

The Taoist priests were asked to perform this ritual by the relatives of the deceased, and this happened because the relatives did not want their dead become wandering and hungry ghosts. In order to avoid this dangerous situation, the correct thing to do is to bring the soul to the place she or he has to go: the ancestors' tablet[10]. This example shows that the ancestors' tablets are not only considered as a symbol made in order to remember or commemorate the deceased. The tablets are where the soul of the deceased person lives, they are linked with the complex cosmology that underlies most of everyday activities that constitute the life of most Taiwanese people. It is important to remember that ancestors differ from ghosts only because they have descendants who take care of them.

In the tradition and cosmology of the Taiwanese popular religion, those who already left, who presently live in, and who will in the future live in this world, share the same lifetime and the same existential world. This belief influences the concept of family, which thus encompassed those who currently live and those who already left this world: the ancestors.

In Taiwan, there are annual ceremonies, like the Spring Festival or the Qingming festival, where the ancestors are revered at their site of burial. However, on ordinary days, ancestors are revered at home. During the first year following the death of a relative, usually, a stick of incense is burnt every day, and rice is offered every day in honor of the dead. Prayers need to be addressed to the ancestors every day, otherwise if the departed souls are not revered; it is believed they will cause evil effects on their living kin. After the first anniversary of the death, a stick of incense is daily offered, but not more rice. Thereafter, rice and food are offered for the birthday and the anniversary of the death of the ancestor.

In the Catholic world, the situation is different. The reverence for ancestors at home was allowed only after the Second Vatican Council (1962-65), so people who converted before that time were not allowed to put a traditional ancestor's shrine in their home. And it is important to remember that until 1949 the only Catholic missionaries present on the island were the Dominicans, who were completely against "the cult of ancestors".

A priest told me that before the Second Vatican Council, people who wanted to be baptized – and so enter the community of the Church – had to burn their ancestors' tablets as well as any portrait of Confucius, or images of their gods. Even though the situation changed after the Second Vatican Council, many people did not want to put their ancestors' tablets

---

10. 林瑋嬪 Wei-ping Lin, "鬼母找女婿," 19–20.

6 Gods, Ghosts, and the Ancestors

Figure 4: Ancestor Tablets in the Jilin Road Church, Taipei

back in their homes, because they felt the position of the Church was not fully understood. "If when I was converted the priest ordered me to burn my ancestors' tablets, why must we now put them again in our home?"
Maybe because of this, I did not see ancestors' shrines in many of the believers' homes that I visited. Nevertheless, sometimes this absence is full of meaning. Father Martin told me that one day he received the visit of two parishioners, a young family who had recently been converted. They told Father Martin that "now we know that we cannot put these things (the ancestors' tablets) in our home, but we do not dare to throw them away, so please, help us to solve this problem". The priest told me that the tablets are still in Belgium in a museum of his congregation.

In some other parishes such as the San Dominic Evangelization Centre in Taipei (Jiling Road) the Catholic faithful took their ancestors' tablets directly to the Church, where the priest organized a properly respectful place to keep them (Fig. 4).

One of the situations I encountered during my fieldwork was that most believers are women, and very often in their families, only these women converted, while their families still believe in the practices of the popular religion. Listening to many priests, it is quite common that both boys and girls attend catechism classes, but when they must make a decision about their baptism, boys usually renounce being baptized because of the pressure of their families who generally do not agree with the conversion of their son. The situation seems different as far as women are concerned: in the case of a thirty-forty-year-old woman, it seems family members do not put as much pressure on them regarding baptism.

This phenomenon is certainly related to the fact that, traditionally, if a son survived the first years of his life, he was automatically recognized as a member of his father's line, and so is entitled to a place on his father's ancestral altar. Whereas, A daughter can never be granted this privilege because women acquire membership in the family lineage only through marriage. From her father's point of view, a daughter is an outsider. She can achieve the right to a place on his altar only by marrying a man who agrees to reside uxorilocally[11]. Ahern points out this fact when interviewing her informants: they told her that a daughter "does not belong to us. From birth on, girls are meant to belong to other people. They are supposed to die in other people's house"[12].

Based on these concepts, it is possible to understand the situation of the Catholic Church in Taiwan, where most believers are women. The fact must be noted that a woman may be allowed by her family to participate in the activities of the Church, but after the marriage sometimes, the husband may not allow the wife to attend these activities.

Mrs. Wang was a married forty-year-old woman. I met her only once at the Resurrection church; according to the other believers she was once a very active parishioner, but after that first time, I did not meet her again at the church. Sometime later, I met her on the street. She was helping a museum committee that wanted to open a museum about the history of the Wanhua district. She invited me to visit the museum and we started to talk. I asked her why she did not come to the church for the Sunday Mass for such a long time, and she told me that she was now very busy at home as well as with this new committee. The following Sunday, when I told the other parishioners about my meeting with Mrs. Wang, they told me that the real problem was that her husband did not allow her to participate to the Church activities. When a woman gets married, she became a member of a specific ancestor line. It is common to find Catholic women that go to the market because "today it is the death anniversary of my father-in-law and we must *bai* (拜) him. Therefore, I bought a lot of things because I want to prepare his favorite food".

Catholic Believers who were converted after the Vatican Council generally still have the traditional ancestors' shrine in their houses, and some old believers reinstalled this shrine in their homes after the Council. According to my fieldwork data, there are multiple reasons that lead these people to have an ancestor's shrine in their home.

Mister Guo is a seventy-year-old parishioner. He was converted at the age of twenty and married a Catholic woman. When he heard that I was doing my research on the cult of ancestors, he invited me to his home for dinner to show me his ancestors' shrine. He told me that he got an ancestors'

---
11. Wolf, "Gods, ghosts, and ancestors," 148.
12. Ahern, *The Cult of the Dead in a Chinese Village*, 127.

shrine only after the death of his father. At that time, he looked at how other people made their ancestors' tablets and shrine, so he carefully made his own. Carefully because as a Catholic he did not want to commit any heresy. Mister Guo's shrine looked like a traditional one, but at the center of it – where images of deities are traditionally put – there was a cross and an image of Jesus. The ancestor's tablet was on the left side of the shrine where, traditionally, it must be. On the tablet, along with the family surname, a cross was painted. He also showed me that in the genealogical book (*zupu* 族譜), starting with him, every member of the family must write the day of baptism and the Christian name (*shenmin* 聖名) besides the name and birthday. Mister Guo told me that a lot of newly converts did not want an ancestors' shrine in their house, but he was convinced that he needed an ancestors' shrine in order to let other Taiwanese people know that the Catholic religion is a Chinese local religion.

This type of argument was shared by Mister Gao, who told me that he had an ancestors' shrine at home in order to let other people know that Catholicism is a Chinese religion. He reinforced this statement by arguing that Jesus, who was born in the Middle East, could be considered to be an oriental character, and that the Christian Faith is universal.

One of the elements that Mister Gao pointed out was that after his conversion he, and consequently his family, felt freer than when they were believers in the Taiwanese popular religion. The fundamental reason for this had to do with the relationship with the ancestors: "as Catholics, we must not be afraid of them." He told me some interesting anecdotes regarding the relationships between the Catholic faithful and non/Catholic Taiwanese people. For example, when a Taiwanese falls down in front of someone else's house, they must go to the shaman of the temple in order to expel the "dirty things" (usually ghosts) of that house from their body. However, when people fall down in front of a Catholic's house, they do not have to go to the temple, because there are no ghosts in that house. When he bought his house, the neighbors told him that the *fengshui* of the house was not good, but when they saw the cross and the images of Jesus hanging on the wall, they told him: "Are you Christian? In this case you can buy this house because for you Christians there are no such problems". According to mister Gao, Taiwanese people know very well that the life of a Catholic or Christian believer (信耶穌的人) is more free and easy than their own life, but people don't want to convert themselves because they are still afraid of their ancestors.

Another interesting encounter was with Mister Li. He was a seventy-year-old parishioner. In doing this interview, a translator helped me, because Mister Li did not speak Chinese fluently, so sometimes he preferred to express himself in Taiwanese. His home was very interesting, the drawing room (客廳), just in front of the main door, was reserved for a big table that functioned as an ancestors' altar (Fig. 5a). A big cross was hanging on the wall, just over the ancestors' tablet. On two large plates were incised two sentences drawn from the Mass liturgy (the first two sentences of the Gloria "Glory to God in the highest and peace on earth to men of goodwill"). A cross was on the ancestor's tablet (Fig. 5b).

(a) (b)

Figure 5: The Altar (a) and the Ancestors' Tablet (b) of Mr. Li, Taipei

This type of disposition of the ancestor's altar is exactly the same as in the traditional Taiwanese home, the *sanheyuan* (三合院), where the ancestors stand in the center of the drawing room just in front of the main door. Mister Li told me that he still prayed to the ancestors by burning sticks of incense in front of the altar and that he had kept the ancestors' tablet as a remembrance, a memory of his ancestors because he knew the soul of his ancestor was not inside the tablets.

According to the Cardinal of Kaohsiung Paul Shan, in 2001 the Catholic Church in Taiwan celebrated the "Congress of the new century and of the new Evangelization" in order to define the pastoral work for the new century. In this congress, the importance of the lay members in the life of the Church was stressed. The attention was therefore put on the family because the family must be witnesses to faith, charity, and hope. The result of this congress was that families were asked to reserve a corner of their house for "Christian symbols", in order to create a religious atmosphere in the family[13]. Probably for this reason many Drawing Rooms (客廳) of Catholics' homes, have visual symbols of the Catholic faith, such as images of Jesus, the Blessed Virgin Mary, the Cross, or the Bible. It is interesting to note that, besides, these sacred images very often there are pictures of more recent ancestors. Like a modern version of the traditional ancestors' shrine.

---

13. Meldrum, *A Cardinal Comes of Age*.

6 Gods, Ghosts, and the Ancestors

At this point, we must point out some careful considerations. The Chinese religion is inseparable from the entire spectrum of discourses and texts through which meaning is produced, reproduced, and fought for, and in which individuals create themselves socially and culturally. In addition to written and printed texts, this spectrum includes all kinds of rituals, shamanism, architecture, economic transactions, knowledge, and even daily conversations[14]. In this way this spectrum of discourses plays the function of the rules that arrange the everyday life of the Taiwanese people, or to make a pun using another metaphor, these are the "Weberian" webs of meanings. Paraphrasing Weber, man is a prisoner of the web of meaning that he himself made, therefore every little and apparently meaningless change hides a lot of meanings that in some ways regulate human conduct and choices. For example, in the specific case of the reverence for Ancestors', there are several rules that a person must follow in order to make a correct ancestors' shrine, rules which concern how to write ancestors' tablets. Therefore the arrangement of the shrine, the position of the image of the deity and the ancestors' tablets on the shrine, the number of Chinese characters which are written on the tablet, the form of the incense pot put in front of the deity of the home or in front of the ancestors' tablets; all these things embody very deep spiritual meaning.

The display of a shrine is an interesting point; there are several rules which control how the shrine and the table must be made. According to these rules, the image of the god of the home must be put at the center of the shrine, while (from the point of view of a person who stands in front of the shrine)[15] the ancestors' tablets must be put on the left part of the shrine. Of course, there are exceptions, but in fact, this is considered the right way to arrange the house shrine. An interesting point is that many Catholic shrines still follow the same rules and patterns; the god image on the center is substituted by that of Jesus or the Blessed Virgin Mary and on the left side comes the ancestors' tablet.

In a home where all family members are Catholic, the husband, a university professor uxorically married, told me that they have an ancestors' shrine in order to demonstrate to non-believers that the Catholic religion allows these practices. As they showed me, the central part of the shrine was occupied by a painting of Jesus and beside it, there was a little statue of Mary. The tablet was located on the left side of the sacred images. On the tablet, belonging to the maternal lineage, a cross was painted. They told me that this is the correct way to paint a Catholic ancestors' tablet. But on the other hand, we have different arrangements for the shrine, and some of them do not seem to follow the above-mentioned rules. In another home, I found the ancestors' shrine in the Drawing Room, in front of the main door, and the ancestors' tablet was put in the middle of the shrine.

---

14. P. Steven Sangren, *History and Magical Power in a Chinese Community* (Stanford: Stanford University Press, 1987), 166.

15. I will keep this point of view for all descriptions of ancestors' shrines.

6.2 Ancestors

Another family invited me to see their ancestors' shrine. It was a traditional one, (the husband had converted only a few years ago) there were no sacred images and the ancestors' tablets stood at the center. In front of the table, there were two little cups full of wine.

(a) (b)

Figure 6: Detail of the altar of the ancestors of Mr. Li (a) and Mr. Zhang (b), Taipei

It is interesting to note how the incense pots put in front of the ancestors' tablet or in front of the god (or gods) of the home are differentiated by some important symbols. The first difference between these two incense pots is that the god's is bigger than the ancestors' incense pot, another meaningful difference concerns the fact that the ancestors' incense pot has two handles called "ears" (耳), while no handles are present on the god's incense pot. Furthermore, I found some homes in which this type of tradition – a tradition dictated by a precise cosmology – was respected, while I found other homes where the ancestors' incense pot was similar to the traditional god's incense pot. These different pots are described in figures 6a and 6b. Furthermore, the numbers of characters that must be written on the ancestors' tablet are subject to some rules. A believer told me that when he did his ancestors' tablet, after the permission of the Church, he wrote the characters according to a tradition for which there are a series of five Chinese characters, life, oldness, illness, death, and suffering (生, 老, 病, 死, 苦)[16], which are arranged in a cyclical way. Generally, some basic information, like who made and offered the tablet, the surname of the lineage, and

---

16. These concepts are linked to the Buddhist concept of Duḥkha (translated in Chinese as 八苦), commonly translated as "suffering", "pain," or "unhappiness," is an important concept in Buddhism, Jainism and Hinduism. Its meaning depends on the context and may refer more specifically to the "unsatisfactoriness" or "unease" of mundane life when driven by craving/ grasping and ignorance.

the date on which the tablet was completed, are written on the ancestors' tablets. This information is commonly written in three vertical lines. The writing on the table cannot exceed six or seven characters. In this way the last character will be linked with a bad symbol like illness or death, so the right numbers of characters are six or seven, eleven or twelve, sixteen or seventeen, and so on, in other words, the characters linked with the good meaning of life or oldness. It is important that the sum of the three lines of characters follow the above-mentioned rules. In addition, the height and the width of the tablet follow this type of rule. Knowing these rules, allows people to immediately understand if a tablet is made in the correct way, or if the man did not follow the rules, and therefore the right tradition. For example, during my fieldwork, I was able to see that while some believers made their ancestors' tablets in a way that did not agree with these rules, other Catholics did. Why this? Why are there so many differences among ways to display the ancestors' shrine? Why did some people still follow the "traditional rule" while other believers ignored them?

A possible answer was given to me by an old believer. He was baptized at the age of twenty, and then he married a woman who was born into a traditional Catholic family. He explained to me many things about his conversion and about the traditions of Popular Religion because he had taken part in many temple festivals during his adolescence, notably helping the temple shaman during the performance of some rituals. When he answered my questions, his wife told me that it was the first time she understood the meanings of many practices of the Taiwanese popular religion, like burning paper money at the grave, or during the first or the fifteenth day of the lunar month. Her husband told me "you see? This is the Old Catholic faithful situation. They don't know the meaning of these rituals, but they still do it just because they saw their neighbors perform it."

This is, in my view, the main point. Some believers do not know the meaning of these rituals, but they still perform them. They do it because they were born and grew up in a specific cultural context. Considering culture as a web of meanings, it is clear that the believers live their lives and perform such religious acts within this web. A web is made not only by the symbols that they know but by symbols that they do not know: symbols that are in some ways real and visible in the behavior of neighbors, relatives, and friends. Taiwanese Catholics are living inside two symbolic systems: they arbitrarily use these symbols, sometimes in their original way, sometimes adapting them to the new symbolic universe, in order to find peace and harmony in their everyday life.

To give a concrete example, the two ancestors' shrine shown in figures eight and nine are not in accord with the traditional way to make and display an ancestors' shrine. The ancestors' tablet stands at the center of the shrine at the place traditionally occupied by the image of a deity. On the other hand, while the first shrine does not follow the traditional rule concerning the ancestors' incense pot, the second still follows these rules.

6.2 Ancestors

Of more significance, the tablet of Fig. 7a shows the character *ling* (靈位) instead of the traditionally used *shen* (神位), as shown by the Fig. 7b.

(a)　　　　　　(b)

Figure 7: Detail of the ancestor tablets of Mr. Li (a) and Mr. Zhang (b), Taipei

It is possible to note that, while the first incense pot does not have any handle (Fig. 6a) – which according to the tradition means that the incense pot is for the gods' home – the second incense pot has "two ears" (Fig. 6b). At the same time, figure number 7a shows us nine characters all written in a unique line, while figure 7b shows us three lines of characters with seven characters on the first line, twelve on the second, and seven in the third, as the traditional tablets must be made.

　　In many Catholic homes, families display the symbols of their faith. In many living rooms, there is a small altar full of religious objects, like crosses, images of Jesus, or Mary (often both are present), the Bible or Gospel, and the Holy Rosary. Sometimes in these types of domestic altars, pictures of the most recent dead ancestors are present, generally parents but pictures of the wife or husband.

As I discovered, the presence of a place inside the home to show the Christian symbols, and consequently their own faith, was encouraged by the Episcopal Conference of Taiwan. The bishops asked the believers to decorate their living room and their homes with Christian symbols, in harmony with the Jubilee of the year 2000[17]. During my research, the parish priest showed me the rules that the believers have to follow when making an ancestor

---

17. Meldrum, *A Cardinal Comes of Age*.

6 *Gods, Ghosts, and the Ancestors*

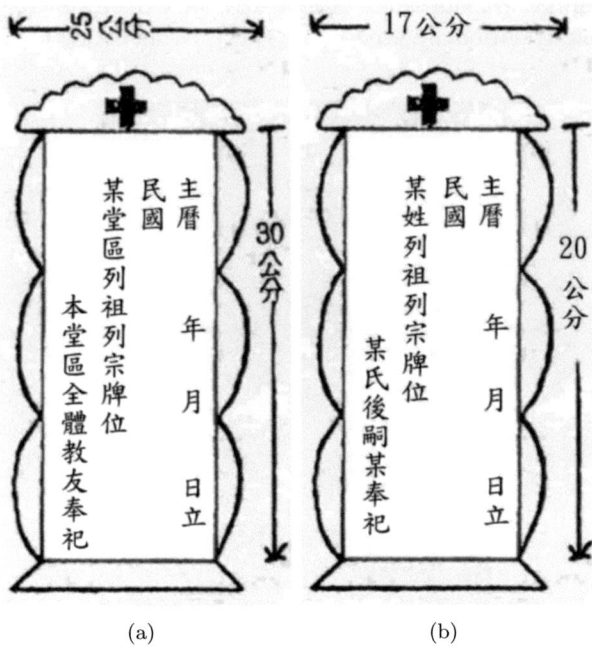

(a)   (b)

Figure 8: Outline of the tablet for the Parish (a) and for the deceased parishioner (b)

tablet, rules concerning the length, the width, the way they must write on the tablet, and concerning how high and large the tablet must be (Figures 8 a and b, Source: 殯葬禮儀)[18].

The interesting thing is that these procedures follow the traditional rules, but in this case, there are other parameters to be followed, like painting a red cross on the tablet. Basic traditional rules are followed by the Catholic Church authorities (Figures 8 a and b), such as the number of characters, the width, and the height, all these rules follow the tradition, which as we saw means following the symbols and the meaning assigned to them by the Taiwanese popular religion. These examples above mentioned could be considered one more proof that man lives within a web of meaning, inside a symbolic system that we call culture. Even if a person embracing a new religious faith enters in this way inside a new symbolic system, his (or her) previous web of meaning that we call culture is still real and present. Sometimes because people have knowledge – as the believer who told me about the five characters cycle – or sometimes because they saw their neighbors' conduct like the old believer told me.

On the other hand, the Church allows the use of the ancestors' tablets and indicates rules to the believers, which represents links with the cosmol-

---

18. 中國主教團禮儀委員會Bishop Conference of China, 殯葬禮儀 (Taipei: Xiuding, 1989).

ogy of the popular religion, drawing a complex and interesting phenomenon. Because without a deep knowledge of the meaning embodied in these above-mentioned symbols, it is very easy to make a mistake. To use a metaphor, we can say that the Church allows the believers to continue using the traditional meaning/ signifier of these above-mentioned signs, but stresses the different meanings (signified) that the Catholic tradition brought. To try to understand this phenomenon will be the objective of the next pages. The Catholic conceptions of ancestors cannot be related only to the presence (or the absence) of the ancestor's tablets. Other facts and aspects can help us understand in more detail this interesting phenomenon.

Miss Li was a fifty-year-old parishioner. She was one of the more regular and active parishioners. She was the third of five children, four daughters, and one son. All the components of the family, starting with the daughters, were baptized, except the son, who still takes care of the ancestors' shrine. The family embraced the Catholic faith in the years following the end of the Second World War; she told me how the priest helped her and her family through the support of the American charity Caritas, help that consisted of flour, milk powder, and school education. After their baptism, the children were allowed to enter for free in a Catholic school. As I wrote above, after the daughters, the father and the mother received baptism (Chap 4). The actual situation is that the son, who was not baptized, and who after the death of the parent continues to take care of the ancestors' tablets, is still involved in the practices of the Taiwanese popular religion.

The baptism in order to receive the Caritas food and other help (especially for the children), the priest who preferred quantity instead of the quality of baptized people, the belief in the physical needs of the ancestors, and the contingent situation of poverty: it seems clear that the mediation between these different influences and motivations built a process led by cultural, cosmological and practical compromises. More interestingly, this case shows how the conception of ancestors is deeply rooted in the Taiwanese culture, the ancestors are felt as near and present, in other words, they still live with their progeny apart from their affiliation to another religion.

Another interesting case was that of Long Qi, an undergraduate student whose father died some years ago. He told me that he and his sister were baptized after they met a priest who came from the United States. When his father died, the mother asked them to go with her to the temple to visit the medium (*tongling* 通靈). At that time Long Qi was already baptized, but because of something that occurred the night after the death of his father, he decided to go with his mother. The fact that I am referring to is linked to a Hakka (客家) belief. The young student told me that there are beliefs according to which the soul of a recently departed can take the appearance of an Imperial Moth (a type of nocturnal butterfly). The night after his father's death, an imperial moth entered the house and landed just on his sister's leg, and even when they tried to let it fly out, the butterfly did not want to leave the leg of the sister. For Long Qi that butterfly was indubitably the soul of the father. When he arrived at the medium temple with his mother and his sister, the medium asked for the name and the address of the deceased. Because they had only recently moved from their old home to a new one situated in Taizhong (台中), Long Qi's mother gave the new address to the medium, but the medium could not find any spirit to communicate with. Therefore, she gave the old address, and the father, through the medium, started to answer the questions of the woman, while Long Qi and his sister were standing behind her. When they heard the words of the medium, all family members were convinced that it was really the father who was talking. In addition, in this case, my intention is to stress the fact that the ancestors are still felt as alive by their descendants, because of the importance of the "cultural roots", but because of the importance of the context in which a person lives his everyday life. Long Qi is a very faithful believer, but he really believed the words of the medium, even if this type of thing conflicted with the fundamental doctrine of his new faith. When he told me his experience, he particularly used expressions like "I don't know how this thing could be possible but things really happened this way" or "I know that this could be explained as a psychological event or in other ways, but we really felt that it was my father speaking."

The ancestors are considered alive and present for most of the believers that I met, and for this reason, some of them used elements of the new religion according to traditional ways to solve troubles that were believed to be linked with ancestors, like offering a Mass for them or, as in the case of Long Qi, directly going to the temple and asking a medium.

The first consideration that could be raised in the interpretation of these experiences could be that within the Catholic Church, there are different ways to consider the ancestors. There are believers who still have a traditional ancestors' shrine to prove the localization of the Catholic religion and others who do not want this kind of thing in their home because they are afraid of it, as in the case of the young couple who gave the ancestors' tablet to Father Martin. There are more different cases, like that of a girl who was baptized in France where she lived for a long time and did not want to know anything about the "ancestors' tablets or whatever" because she felt this kind of thing was just superstition.

6.2.1 Ancestors and the Catholic Church

One of the principal points linked to the belief system in the ancestors is that they still are present and generate significant pressure not only on the worldview of Catholic believers but also on the evangelization process carried out by the Church. According to the testimonies that I collected, it seems to me that there is an effort of the Church to present Christ as the first ancestor (the first who resurrected and the first who defeated death). The problem arises because the believers still use their own cultural system to explain the new faith, and according to it, Christ is God, not an ancestor, because ancestors are more linked with the home, with the property, with the parentage, and the descent.

People in Taiwan live immersed in a cultural system that molds every act of their everyday life. As consequence, according to their personal situation, contingency, and needs, they arbitrarily choose a symbol able to resolve a practical situation, as in the case of Miss Li's parents, where they were able to harmonize symbols belonging to different traditions and the contingent situation of their lives. Even when they accept the re-sematization, the reconfiguration of their belief system made by the Church, they continue to refer to the old meaning of these symbols as in the case of Mister Guo and Mister Gao, who stressed their freedom from their ancestors, proving in this way the existence of this category of supernatural beings. The problem of the relationship with ancestors is still real for them because they still participate in the everyday experiences of their neighbors, friends, or relatives, but by embracing the new faith, these problems could be resolved.

Even if these types of problems could arise again, believers very often still use their traditional way to solve them, but applied with new forms, like for example going to Church and asking a Mass in honor of their ancestors. As I said above, I was a witness to this kind of case: believers I had never met before in more than four years, suddenly appeared in the middle of the week in order to offer a Mass for their ancestors. The common practice of popular religion to go to the temple in order to solve problems, a practice that is built on a deep and strong cosmology, is seen by some of the Taiwanese Catholic people as the natural way to face problems. Therefore it asserted that this is the natural way to conceive life and the relationships with the supernatural world (that for Taiwanese people is absolutely not supernatural, but irrefutably natural) molds the Catholic's way to relating to the new symbols (or new interpretation) brought by the new religion.

This situation of compromise is helped by the conduct of the Church by trying to implement some practices in order to align herself with the local customs and culture. For example, I mentioned the fact that some Catholics still burn paper money at their ancestor's and deceased parents' grave. This practice is officially prohibited by the Church, but as a Brother told me, there are many Catholics that still burn paper money at the cemetery because they see other people do it. In order to contrast with this practice, special paper money with sacred images called Resurrection Paper (*fuhuozhi* 復活紙), is sold in Catholic stores (Fig. 9a and b).
Their purpose is to offer a substitute to the traditional Deep Paper, the Taiwanese *bongzua* (*wusezhi* 五色紙 or *huangseguzhi* 黃色古紙), which are placed on the graves in concordance with the Tomb Sweeping Festival, and they mean that the grave where they are placed were already cleaned and worshiped (Fig. 10).

6 *Gods, Ghosts, and the Ancestors*

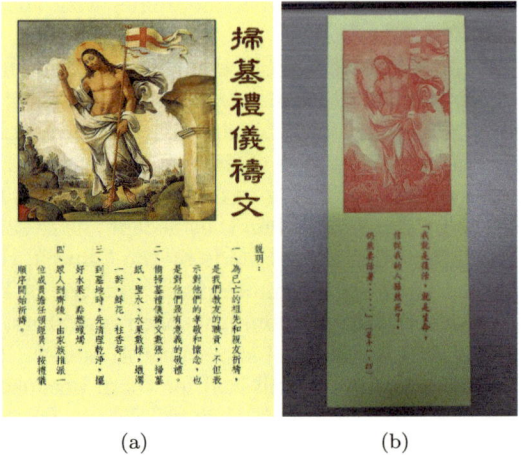

(a)   (b)

Figure 9: fuhuozhi 復活紙

Figure 10: Resurrection Papers on a Traditional Tomb, Taichung

But these papers have another meaning, the *Kamhia* (*gaiwa* 蓋瓦) which is related to the conception that the dead in the other world will need a house of his property with all the commodities inside, including money, which will be used by the deceased in the other-world life. Using Resurrection papers – which imply the meaning that the deceased is resurrected, went to heaven, and already became part of God's glory – the Church completely changed the meaning of this habit, but at the same time attest to the structural division of the categories present in the tradition of popular religion. This fact can help me explain how this dialectic process is made of contact and compromise. I say dialectic because it is undisputed that, in this case, there are two cosmologies (or cultural systems) that meet, collide and interact within the space represented by individuals. The believers, although converted, are still linked to the practices of the popular religion of burning paper money at the ancestors' graves, because this money will be used by the ancestors in the other world. The Church forbids it but at the same time attests to the presence of the ancestors permitting to use of the resurrection papers.

6.2.2 Funerals

When does a deceased person become an ancestor? Immediately after death? Must she or he wait for some time? Is it necessary to perform some particular ceremonies? For both religions, there is no clear and univocal answer, but generally speaking, for common people, it is reasonable to fix this term to align and agree with the funeral rites.

In all religions, funerals are a particular event. In part because of the emotional power expressed by these kinds of rites, and because of the social value that they represent. Funerals are key events in the creation of a shared local history for kin and neighbors[19]. More important according to Watson "To be Chinese is to understand, and accept the view, that there is a correct way to perform rites associated with the life-cycle, the most important being weddings and funerals"[20]. Thus, in this view, these kinds of rites take particular and fundamental importance.

To understand the importance of funeral rites in Taiwan, it is necessary to contextualize them from the perspective of the ancestor's rites. For the traditions of both religions, it is after the funeral that the deceased becomes an ancestor, and consequently can be prayed for or revered at home. During my fieldwork, I participated in some catholic funeral ceremonies, but I was able to participate in a funeral ceremony of the Taiwanese popular religion. These kinds of ceremonies, and especially the social context that comes with them, were very well described by eminent scholars like Wolf or Freedman[21]. According to these studies and in accordance with my personal experience, every member of the family must wear a different dress. Traditionally there are five kinds of dress (*wufu* 五服, which comprehend *zhuanshuai* 斬榱, *jishuai* 齊榱, *dagong* 大功, *xiaogong* 小功, *sima* 緦麻), which express the different relationships of the relative with the deceased, and consequently the relations between the relatives. We can thus say that this type of tradition shows the structural scheme of the Chinese family.

Freedman suggests that "The *wufu* (五服) was in principle a category drawn up in regard to a given ego; it could not, therefore, be a discrete

---

19. Lozada, *God Aboveground*.
20. James L Watson, "The Structure of Chinese Funerary Rites: Elementary Forms, Ritual Sequence, and the Primacy of Performance," in *Death ritual in late imperial and modern China*, ed. James L. Watson, Evelyn Sakakida Rawski, and Joint Committee on Chinese Studies (U.S.) (Berkeley: University of California Press, 1988), 3.
21. Arthur P. Wolf, "Chinese Kinship and Mourning Dress," in *Family and kinship in Chinese society*. Ed. Ai-li S Chin et al. (Stanford, Calif.: Stanford University Press, 1970), 189–207; Freedman, *Lineage Organization*.

segment of lineage. But while the term was used to define the range of agnatic[22] kinsmen to whom a given individual was supposed to hold himself closely related and with whom he should cooperate in a number of ways, in another sense it marked out different classes of relatives, both agnatic and otherwise, for the specification of types and duration of mourning due to them; whence the literal meaning of the expression"[23].

In his essay, Arthur Wolf points out that it is an ancient commonplace (and a rather dull one) that Chinese mourning dress reflects kinship relations to the deceased. Wolf, however, analyzes the use of colors and of types of fabric and distinguishes hierarchies of each and every reason for the selection of one as against another in each case. Some mean more than one thing. Wolf discovered two different uses of red: a great-great-grandson wears red as a sign of joy at the deceased having such a long line. A neighbor wears "prophylactic red" against contamination by death[24]. As the argument progresses, Wolf finds that a finer distinction is necessary: "Mourning dress does not reflect generalized kinship statuses, but is rather a reflection or declaration of rights in property (...) Among those mourners who share property rights with the deceased (...) red expresses joy; outside of the family among people who do not share property rights (...) red is worn as a prophylactic"[25]. To summarize, according to Wolf mourning dress does not reflect generalized kinship statuses, but is rather a declaration of rights in the property. Wolf analyzed data only for northern Taiwan, but he provides an approach for the profitable analysis of mourning apparel across China. I don't want to analyze how other scholars analyzed these phenomena, nor to make an analysis of mourning dress in Taiwanese popular religion. I want to show that in the traditional funerals of the Taiwanese popular religion, people put different kinds of clothes on and that these clothes are in some ways related to the family structure. At the end of the funeral ceremony, the specialist in ritual gives the family a temporary ancestor's tablet, a paper one. Traditionally after a year, this paper tablet will be replaced by the wooden tablet, but actually, at least in Taipei city, the specialist and the family, because of the frenetic style of life in modern-day Taiwan, tend to handle this question in six, and sometimes in two, three months. However, the central point is that after the funeral you can obtain a tablet, which attests that your parent has already becomes become an ancestor. Contrariwise, in the Catholic funeral, the familiar relationships shown by dresses are not accentuated. There are clear regulations about the disposition of the family nearby the coffin, concerning how the believers, depending on their degree of relationship with the deceased, must take a

---

22. Agnatic = male/paternal lineage
23. Freedman, *Lineage Organization*, 41.
24. Wolf, "Chinese Kinship and Mourning Dress."
25. Wolf, 196.

position in the church, and about how the deceased must be revered (Fig. 11)[26].

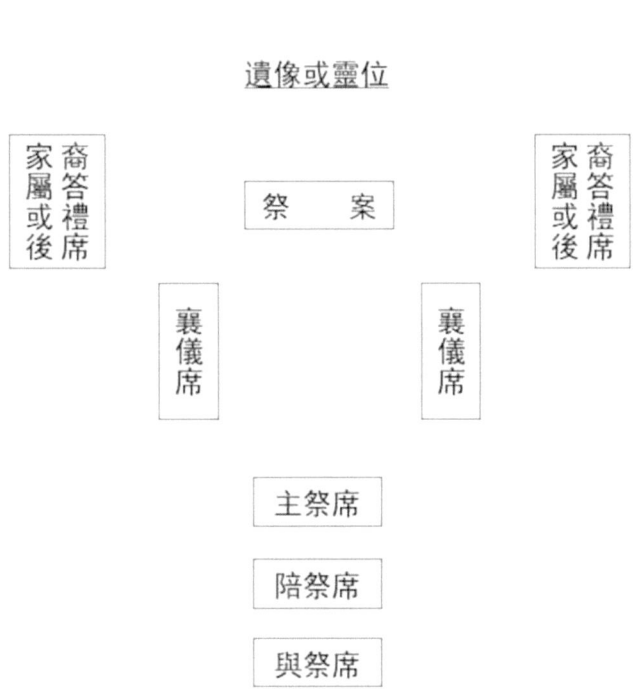

Figure 11: The division of seats inside the church during the funeral. 中國主教團禮儀委員會Bishop Conference of China, 殯葬禮儀 (Taipei: Xiuding, 1989)

Some distinction between the relatives and the group of believers who participated in the funeral is still present, but because the funeral ceremony is incorporated into the rites of the Mass, the whole funeral ceremony assumes a particular meaning. At the traditional Catholic funeral, any member of the family must wear a black dress. As pointed out above, the importance of these funeral rites within the world of Han people must be sought not only on the affective and emotional sides of these manifestations but on the

---
26. 中國主教團禮儀委員會Bishop Conference of China, 殯葬禮儀.

cultural link that is embedded in these ritualized practices[27]. In order to better understand how these rites represent a type of cultural standardization, Watson tried to isolate and point out some essential points from the progress of the funeral rite, that in his view could represent the fundamental and recursive step that must be performed in a Chinese funeral[28] (Watson, 1988:12-13). My goal is to try to compare these "standard" points with the Catholic funeral process as I saw it in Taiwan. Watson recognizes at first the public notification of death by wailing and other expressions of grief. The death must be announced by high-pitched and stereotyped wailing to the neighbors and the community. The author asserts that there is a formal notification, such as the use of the color white to dress and hanging blue lanterns. It seems that high pitch and stereotypical wailing are basic requirements. Especially woman must express their desperation in cries and with a high pitch. And, as I heard, women have to go back to their father's home by walking without shoes in order to show all the pain and grief of the recent death. Watson considers these types of conduct as stereotypical; other people, the neighbors, for example, are expecting this kind of conduct from the relatives of the dead. On the Catholic side, the relatives of the dead are not required to perform these kinds of rites. Since the first period of diffusion of the Church in the Roman Empire, the moment of death was considered a "second birth": the "birth into eternal life" and in some ways the real birth of a Christian believer. Death is the moment on which we will leave this "vale of tears" and on which we finally will meet God in Heaven where we will share his peace and mercy. We live in this world as guests, in transit, but our permanent home, our purpose is to return to our Father's home. Thus, according to these conceptions, the deceased leaves for a better place, and such desperate conduct by his relatives is not necessary. The second point shown up by Watson is linked with the above-mentioned concept of *wufu* (五服). This aspect has already been described exhaustively but there is a significant structural difference between the traditional mourning dresses and the clothes used by the Catholic believers in the Church's ceremonies. A parallel could be built between the different colors of the traditional clothes, as seen in reference to the different degrees of family links with the dead, and the position that the believers take inside the church during the funeral's performance (Fig. 11).

The third point that Watson proposes is the ritualized bathing of the corpse. The author considers this point as an essential feature of the rites. These kinds of practices vary from a full, vigorous scrubbing to a ritualized daubing of the forehead. Watson points out that in some places in south China water was purchased from the deity of a well or a stream; this rite is called "buying water" (*maishui* 買水). This point is very important within the Catholic rites. The sprinkling of holy water on the body of the dead

---

27. Watson, "The Structure of Chinese Funerary Rites: Elementary Forms, Ritual Sequence, and the Primacy of Performance."
28. Watson, 12–13.

is considered an essential part of the funeral rite. According to Catholic tradition and doctrine, the meaning of the sprinkling of holy water is linked with the meaning of baptism, the meaning of Easter, and the resurrection of Christ. Believers and people who attend the funeral are sprinkled by the priest; this symbolizes the union in God between the deceased and those who still live. Both take part in and constitute the Catholic Church.

The fourth point is the transfer of food, money, and goods from the living to the dead. This part of the ritual encompasses all the furniture (house, car, and so on) already discussed above. Watson contends that this kind of performance shows up implicit elements of symbolic communication; this elementary feature of the rites was a concrete expression of the continuing relationship between the living and the dead. As pointed out earlier, at funeral rites of the Catholic Church, offers of food (fruits, rice, and wine) and incense are allowed. According to my experience, these kinds of food offerings are not allowed in all churches, some priests do not allow them. In such cases, only incense and holy water are offered. These practices were debated throughout the history of evangelization in China. The link between these practices and the concept of filial piety (孝) was and is one of the most important factors that persuaded the Church to accept them (事死如事生). On the other hand, the concept of the "Heavenly Jerusalem" also accepts the continuing relationship between living and dead.

The fifth point is the preparation and installation of a soul tablet for the dead. Of course, these rites require the services of a literate person, usually a specialist in ritual. While the Catholic Church allows the presence of the ancestors' shrine and consequently of the ancestors' tablets in the Catholics' homes, no specialist in ritual is necessary to make such ancestors' tablets, because it is believed that there are no souls living inside the tablets. This implies that those who own an old tablet still use it, while some of those who do not have a tablet will make a new one even if they do not have full knowledge of the complex rules which regulate this type of rite.

The sixth point concerns the ritualized use of money and the employment of professionals. The proper conduct of Chinese funerary rites requires the service of specialists who perform ritual acts in exchange for money. According to Watson, the payment of money to specialists was more than a simple monetary exchange, it was a required feature of the rites. The Catholic Church does not recognize any specialist except the priest. The authority of the priest derives from different sources: his studies and the sacrament. It is believed that when a priest is ordained, he is consecrated by a special sacrament. And it is because of this sacrament that he can perform the Catholic rites. In fact, no money is requested by the priest, and usually, people leave a free offering to the priest after the ceremony.

Still following Watson, the seventh point is the music that must accompany the corpse and settle the spirit. Especially, two forms of music play a key role in the structure of funerary rites: high-pitched piping and percussion. The sound of piping accompanies the corpse during critical transitions in the ritual, most notably when physical movement is required.

Music, especially songs and choirs are present in the Catholic ceremony. Music accompanies the entry and the exit of the coffin in the church, but music plays an important function in the key moments of the celebration. In contrast to the traditional funeral, the emphasis is not put on the effective role of the high-pitched instrumental music, but on the meaning of the texts sung: biblical psalms and musical adaptations of biblical texts are sung during the funeral. These songs are all centered on the Resurrection (i.e. John 1,25), the Mercy of God (i.e. psalm 33;136), and the confidence that God brings the dead to a better and peaceful place (i.e. psalm 22).

Sealing the corpse in an airtight coffin is the eighth point in Watson's paper. This action is considered by many Chinese to be the most important feature of the traditional funerary ritual. The ceremonial hammering of nails to seal the corpse within the coffin is a centerpiece of the ritual sequence; these acts are usually performed by the chief mourner or by an invited guest. This is performed at the end of the funeral ritual when the coffin must be carried away. Usually, the coffin is put behind the altar where the picture of the deceased is put, the coffin is opened and at a certain point, the relatives must go to the back in order to see the corpse of their relative. Children and pregnant women are forbidden to pay this visit or to attend the funeral because it is believed that during the funeral many dirty spirits (*huiqi* 穢氣) could be present. These are the type of spirits, which are linked with death and the funeral. They can put in danger the spirits (*po* 魄) of the children because the children's *po* tend to go out of the body. According to Catholic tradition, the body must be put inside an airtight coffin. Traditionally the Church did not allow other practices such as the incineration of the body, the body must be preserved undivided and undamaged because it will resurrect "on the last day", on Judgment Day.

In Taiwan during the Catholic funeral, sometimes the coffin is kept open until the end of the Mass. At this moment believers are invited to come closer to the coffin in order to pay the last tribute to the dead. Here, in my view, there is a clear influence of the Chinese way to perform these rituals. But the great and deep change is symbolized by the fact that while the Chinese ceremony allows only the relatives to give their homage to the deceased, the Catholic tradition extends the concept of family, and allows all the believers to pay homage to the deceased, who is addressed as brother/sister throughout the ceremony. After all the believers (at least those who want to) have seen the dead, the coffin is closed and carried away to the cemetery. Talking with many parishioners, I discovered that many believers, especially if freshly converted, do not want to see the corpse of the dead because of the concept of *huiqi* introduced above. An old parishioner told me that "we must not push these new converted to see the dead, because they are afraid (害怕) of it, when I was converted, I was afraid too."

The ninth point presented by Watson is the mandatory removal of the coffin from the community. This expulsion is the last formal act in the sequence of funerary rites. In the Catholic performance of the funeral, the removal of the coffin is the last part of the rites. The priest with the relatives and sometimes other parishioners accompanies the coffin to the grave, there they recite some prayers and sing songs and the priest sprinkles holy water on the grave and on the coffin. The interesting point is that, apart from these last rituals performed at the grave, all the Catholic funeral rites are embodied in the rite of the Mass, in this way the funeral is symbolically embodied with the life, the death, and the Resurrection of Jesus, which is celebrated within the Mass. This performance is, thus, a way to let the deceased person share Jesus' Resurrection, His eternal life, and joy.

Funerals in the Resurrection Church

During my fieldwork, I attended the funeral of a believer. An eighty-year man was unexpectedly hit by a stroke. I was able to visit him at the hospital, and just two days later he passed away. Because he was an old believer and his son and daughters were very active in the activities of the parish (the elder daughter was the organist in the Resurrection Church) many people participated in his funeral. So, the ceremony was performed not in the Dali Resurrection Church, because it was too small, but at the Holy Rosary Church in Wanda road, a Church administrated by the priests of the C.I.C.M.

The open coffin was put in front of the altar and a large picture of the deceased was put in front of the coffin. On the sides of the coffin were two benches, one on the right side and the other one on the left side. The bench on the left side (tiger part) of the coffin was reserved for the wife, the daughters, the daughter-in-law, and the granddaughter. In other words, the bench was reserved for the female part of the family. On the right side (Dragon Part) were seated the male members: the son, the son-in-law, and the grandson. Both female and male members dressed in black vests.

The funeral ceremony was celebrated within the rite of the Mass, at the end of which incense sticks, fruits, wine, and flowers were offered by the son with three ritual bows, while other relatives were standing behind him. After the son performed the rites, everybody, in order of their degree of relationship with the deceased or with the family, performed the same rites. After the Mass, the female members of the family took the seats of the male members. At this time the believers would go to the coffin for a last greeting or prayer and then give their condolence to the family of the deceased who would be seated in a line and all the believers would shake hands with them.

Every parish priest performs these rites in his own way or according to the parishioners' request. During my fieldwork, I participated in a very singular funeral. An active and old Resurrection Church parishioner, a woman more than seventy years old, passed away. Her sons were baptized at a young age, but for many reasons, when they grew up none of them continued with the rites and activities of the church. At the time of their mother's funeral, they practiced the Taiwanese popular religion.

Because their mother was so active in the parish, they decided to perform a Catholic funeral inside the church; but at the same time, they prepared a *hú-lín-cuò* (糊靈厝, the Taiwanese *go-lín-tzù*) for their mother and asked the priest the permission to put it inside the church. The *go-lín-tzù* is a house made of paper, inside the house, there are all types of furniture and other commodities, like TV, phone and mobile phone, car, air conditioners, etc (Fig. 12). More recently I saw dogs made of paper, notebooks, and other objects of contemporary technology. This kind of house, with all the paper-made material, is usually burnt after the rites of the funeral.

Figure 12: The Taoist paper house inside the Church of the Resurrection, Taipei

The priest allowed them to put the paper house in the church for the funeral. He explained his decision stating that if he had not allowed them to put the paper house in the church, then perhaps they would not have organized a Catholic funeral for their mother. He prepared a Mass, and specifically a homily, based on a metaphorical dialectic with the paper house.

The Gospel that he chose was based on the concept of the Father's House, which in the metaphor of Jesus means Heaven, where all men will go after death: "In my Father's House there are many dwelling places. If there were not, would I have told you that I am preparing a place for you? And if I go and prepare a place for you, I will come back and take you to myself, so that where I am you will be. Where (I) am going you know the way." Thomas said to him, "Master, we do not know where you are going; how can we know the way?" Jesus said to him, "I am the way and the Truth and the life. No one comes to the Father except through me. If you know me, then you will know my Father. From now on you know him and have seen him" (John, 2-7).

After the Gospel reading, and during the homily, the priest accentuated the metaphorical character of his intentions. He spoke about the paper house, which according to him was a symbol, and as a symbol must bring meaning, and the meaning of the paper house is that the sons hope that their mother now will be in a comfortable and beautiful place. He continued explaining that the paper house is a tradition, but not the real place where their mother will go, because the real place is the "Father's House", where Jesus already has prepared a place for all of us. Then the sons offered incense sticks with fruit, wine, and flowers. After the Mass they waited until the incense sticks burned to half, then went to the cemetery, bringing with them the paper house to burn at their mother's grave.

Thus I saw, in the same parish, two completely different ways to perform funeral ceremonies, both were performed inside the church, and within the rite of the Mass, but they emphasize different aspects of the ritual of the funeral and different ways that different priests have to face similar ritual problems. The first funerary ceremony stressed the egalitarian character of the cultural universe of the Catholic Church. Despite the funeral ceremony of the Taiwanese popular religion, where every relative must wear a different color and different forms of dress, the funeral of the Catholic Church requires that every close relative must wear black clothes. There are no distinctions between older or younger sons or between son and son-in-law. Some distinction is still found in the spatial separation inside the Church between men and women and between different degrees of kinship, differences that disappear at the end of the Mass when all the family of the deceased sits together. As seen above, this aspect of the ceremony tends to stress the equality of every person before God. Because before God we are all brothers and sisters. Apart from the separation by sex, (such separation is already present in the Bible), there are no clear distinctions. This implies that the son and son-in-law of the deceased can, in the funerary ceremony, wear similar clothes.

The second ceremony was integrally arranged in a dialectic relationship with the symbols of the popular religion: the paper house, the Gospel, the homely, and so on. The fact that the priest allowed the believer's sons to put the paper house inside the church was criticized by some parishioners, asserting that in this way people cannot distinguish between the two religions. But many believers agreed with the priest, because "at least in this way Miss Ma (the deceased mother) was able to have a Catholic funeral."

It seems to me that these two cases of funerals, celebrated by the same priest in different contexts, can help comprehension of how not only common believers choose symbols in order to solve a problem or in order to adapt themselves to some particular situations. The priest used the same approach choosing the more appropriate symbols in order to resolve a particular situation, or in order to make clear his message that the more understanding and accommodating the Church was, then the more inclusive the Church would be.

In conclusion, it is principally the category of ancestors that stimulates and creates a dialogue, a dialectical process between the cosmologies of the two religions. This process is made by compromises, prohibitions, common sense, and personal interpretation of the doctrinal rules. A dialogue made within the person, which – as I stressed above – could be a Taiwanese Catholic, or a foreign priest as well as the relationships between them, relationships that are a historical result of communications, choices, tensions, and negotiations.

6.3 Ghosts

Ghosts (*gui* 鬼) are the third category of supernatural beings that enliven Chinese cosmology. They are souls that have left the body too fast, because of a rough death, like suicide, a car crash, or maybe drowning and so on. But specifically, all the people who died without descendants, are considered as *gui*, and without people who care for them, providing for their prayers, food, money, etc., when they are in the spirit world; in other words, those who have no descendants to revere/venerate them as ancestors. These ghosts usually are active after sunset, when they come out in order to find something to eat because there are no people who either care about them or care for them. This definition of gui, gives a deeper understanding of why sometimes parents are so averse to the fact that their son wants to convert and embrace a new faith. The fundamental point is that according to the Taiwanese people's common knowledge, Christians cannot pray to their own ancestors, and their concept of Christianity includes both Protestants and Catholics. People really believe that if a son embraces a new faith, they will become a ghost rather than an honored ancestor. These spirit presences seem very real to them, and many times are believed to be responsible for the unluckiest events that happen in the everyday life of the majority of Taiwanese people. Because of ghosts, people burn paper money and make offerings at least two times a month, at home and in front of their stores, restaurants, banks, convenience stores, etc., those who work with the Stock Exchange every day burn paper money and offer incense to these *gui*.

6.3 Ghosts

During my stay in Taiwan, I observed many times the relationships present between Taiwanese people and *gui*. One time I read in the newspaper that a man who was driving on a road that passed through a cemetery in Taipei City was scanned by a radar gun, a small Doppler radar used to detect the speed of cars. The driver complained to the police station; that because of passing through a cemetery area, some *gui* tampered with the radar gun. Another time a friend of mine, who had given birth only a few months before, invited me to take coffee near the university. Around five o'clock in the evening – in Taipei in the winter the sun wanes around five thirty or six o'clock – she told me that she must go back home because at sunset, the *gui* come out and this could be dangerous for the child. And at the school, a schoolmate told me that he was involved in a motorcycle accident when he was passing through a cemetery. He felt like someone was pushing his motorcycle and suddenly he crashed. The time was right at sunset. These are just some experiences that I collected during my stay in Taiwan, but I could tell you many more experiences or episodes that I heard from classmates or friends.

Reading the books that eminent scholars wrote doing research upon popular religion, there are many descriptions of these types of relationships between man and *gui*. These relationships are felt as real and concrete, so concrete that a man could be married to one of these souls, as well described by Wolf[29]. This custom described by Wolf as a "ghost marriage" is still real and absolutely present in Taiwan. One of the first things that my friends told me when I arrived in Taiwan was "please do not pick up anything from the road, especially red packets" (which are put out by relatives to find a man to "marry" a dead girl); And I have watched television programs which presented this phenomenon. What I try to demonstrate here is that these beings are real in the minds of the Taiwanese, people feel their presence and feel they interfere with people's lives. Because of this situation, people still respect and propitiate these ghosts, at least two times a month, especially during the seventh month in the Chinese calendar, the "Month of the Hungry Ghosts". Buddhists, Taoists, and believers of Chinese popular religions believe that during "Ghost Month", the spirits of the dead wander the earth, and the Gates of Hell are said to be opened during this month. Therefore, For one long Lunar month, ghosts are said to roam the Earth; many people told me that they still feel uncomfortable going out at night around the Ghost Festival days. During this dangerous time, they suspend all important activities and decisions. Such as traveling, weddings, moving to a new house, and even swimming are suspended.

The specific Festival of the Hungry Ghosts is on the 15th day of the seventh moon in the Chinese Lunar calendar. On that day families solemnly pay homage to their ancestors and pay Buddhist or Taoist monks (as a charity) to pray for their souls, but at the same moment, they offer food

---

29. Wolf, "Gods, ghosts, and ancestors," 150–151.

in order to propitiate the hungry ghosts that live on the surface of the Earth for that period of time. In this month it is very common, to walk on the streets of Taipei, and see people burning paper money to please the visiting ghosts and spirits, or to see people preparing ritual offerings of food, generally inferior food that is thought good enough for ghosts, such as dried pork rinds or pig head skins. Other activities include buying and releasing miniature paper boats and lanterns on water, which signifies "giving directions to the lost ghosts."

Anthropologists who studied the Taiwanese popular religion described these ghosts as strangers or outcasts[30], and in this way, the author stressed the importance of an inside/outside opposition, where ancestors are prayed to facing towards the inside of the house, and ghosts are prayed to facing towards outside. This concept of *gui* as strangers has been stressed by Weller[31]. Wolf defined them as the supernatural equivalent of bandits, beggars, and other strangers[32], included in the term "stranger" the ancestors from other lineages because according to him the category "ghosts" is always a relative one. Your ancestors are my ghosts, and my ancestors are your ghosts, just as your relatives are strangers to me, and my relatives are strangers to you[33].

Strangers and outsiders. Even if there are other definitions of ghosts made by other scholars, such as "anomalies inside the structure" or "entities without identity"[34], I chose these two descriptions because these represent, in my view, the basic points of divergence between the concept of ghosts of the popular religion and the Catholic point of view about these beings.

What I noticed through the analysis of the Catholic ancestors' rites, the category of *gui* disappeared, both spatially and hierarchically (in Feuchtwang terms). According to Christian cosmology, in fact, all people are equally the object of God's love and mercy, so all people when they will leave this world will meet God and could share in His mercy, or be judged based on their sins. However, in all cases they will find a precise place in another world; they will not remain here in this world. In this way, all the festivals dedicated to the *gui* are irrelevant, they have no reason to be celebrated. On the other hand, the Catholic doctrine considers all people as the children of God. He destined us for adoption to himself through Jesus Christ, in accord with the favor of his will (Ephesians 1,5). As consequence, all people are brothers and sisters, and the concept of the stranger is erased – "there is neither Jew nor Greek, there is neither slave nor free person, there is not male and female; for you are all one in Christ Jesus" (Galatians 3,27-28). In this way, any type of ceremony, with the excep-

---

30. Feuchtwang, "Domestic and communal worship in Taiwan," 127.
31. Robert Weller, *Resistance, Chaos and Control in China: Taiping Rebels, Taiwanese Ghosts and Tiananmen* (University of Washington Press, 1994).
32. Wolf, "Gods, ghosts, and ancestors," 134.
33. Wolf, 173.
34. Sangren, *History and Magical Power in a Chinese Community*, 150, 155.

tion of Tomb Sweeping Day, is performed facing inside, at the church, or at home. No ceremonies or offerings are performed toward the outside, where traditionally are posed the offerings for the ghosts, for the strangers who came from outside. Nevertheless, how it is possible these entities that are felt so concrete and active in Taiwanese everyday life have disappeared from the Taiwanese Catholics' everyday life? There is a sentence quite common among Taiwanese people, "If you believe it, there it will be, but if you do not it will not". I heard this sentence several times when I asked some Catholics about the existence of *gui*, but this kind of answer was not the only one, and more significantly was not the more common.

When I asked Mister Gao if he believed in the existence of ghosts, his answer was "of course *gui* exist!" (*gui dangran shi youde* 鬼當然是有的), and to reinforce this assertion, he started to tell me some stories about *gui* (鬼故事). He told me about an incident that occurred to his friend. He was going to his home when he saw a little boy sitting on a parapet of a bridge. The man asked him what he was doing here at that time, and the little boy answered that he was waiting for his big brother. Calmed by this answer, the man went back to his home. When he arrived home his wife told him that a little boy and his big brother had been found dead in the river, just under that bridge. Mister Gao told me this story very slowly and with great respect, like when he told me other stories about miracles.

A parishioner told me another interesting story; she told me that she had a friend who was able to see these supernatural presences (陰視). This friend told her that the cemeteries in Taiwan are usually "full of people" (which means full of ghosts), but when she went to one Catholic cemetery she did not see anyone. The parishioner told me that after this discovery she felt more confident in her faith. Through these experiences, and despite the concepts mentioned above, for Taiwanese Catholics, these presences still are real, ghosts exist, but it seems that these presences do not have a so strong relationship with the Catholic people.

Miss Tang was a forty-year-old parishioner; I worked with her for a period in 2007. She was the secretary of a Catholic organization and I was helping with some documents in her office and doing some short translations or something else. One day, when we were at the office, she received a phone call. She told me that it was another believer who called her because "someone" saw "someone" around her. This means that maybe a medium or a *Dáng-Ki* told her that some ghosts were following her. I was very surprised because it is already strange that a Catholic would go to the medium, but it was stranger for me that a ghost was believed to be moving around following a person. Miss Tang told me that working in this kind of association; she already knew of many experiences like that. In her opinion people without a strong faith, maybe because of curiosity or maybe in order to receive some help, go to the fortuneteller, *suanmin* (算命), and in this way, they allow these ghosts contact with them. Otherwise, these presences would not be able to contact them. As evidence of this theory, she told me her story. She was the last of four children, her mother went to the *suanmin* in order to choose the best names for the first three children (two girls and one male), while she chose by herself a name for Miss Tang who was the youngest daughter. Because of this, after their conversion, Miss Tang considers her faith more stable and stronger than that of her sisters and brother.

The ghosts still can be real and of course, they can enter into contact with you, even if not so directly. The interesting point is that many believers pointed out the fact that ghosts exist, but because they are Catholics, ghosts do not have any power over them.

Yi Ju was a very young woman, around twenty-three years old. She was baptized in her childhood because her parent was both Catholics. She was very active in the group of youth Catholics, and like many Taiwanese young people, she likes to talk with foreign friends. When she knew what type of studies I was doing, she told me many stories. Yi Ju told me that she heard many "ghost stories" from her parents. She told me about a girl who could see these supernatural beings; her mother was Catholic but because she divorced her husband, the girl, who received baptism, lived with her grandmother, the mother of the father. One day the little girl saw "someone" moving around the grandmother. She was very scared and suddenly she remembered that her mother taught her some Christian prayers. The little girl started to say her prayers and the ghost suddenly disappeared. Then when the grandmother brought the little girl to the temple in order to consult the *suanmin*, after some moments he told the old woman that "sorry I cannot do anything with her because there is a cross on her forehead." After this event, the grandmother started to frequent some of the Church's activities. It is not my intention here to ascertain if these stories are real or not, and neither to demonstrate that people really saw ghosts. My aim is to that the symbolic universe, within which Catholics live, is the same that regulates the lives of the practitioners of popular religion. The experiences that they meet every day are the same experiences that ordinary people meet every day, but according to the new faith, the Catholic faith, these experiences are interpreted differently, using the order made by the new symbolic system.

In this way, the ghosts still are real but they are subjugated to the power of the new symbols. This is in my view one of the most important points of divergence with the theory of Sahlins I previously introduced. People not only still use their original cultural system in order to interpret a new event, but use the new symbolic system to re-interpret the old one. In practice, giving a new order of value to the old symbolic system, ghosts still can be real but believers do not need to offer food or money to them, because God's power in baptism is stronger, Catholics belong to Him, so there is no reason to be afraid of these ghosts. Only if their faith is not strong enough, people, because of their curiosity or whatever, will meet problems. This situation in my view stresses the fact that the complex encounter between two different cultural systems takes place in the space represented by humans. In this space, different symbols belonging to different systems can arbitrarily – according to people's own current situation – be chosen in order to solve problems and troubles that people meet in their everyday life.

Chapter 7

Conclusions

7.1 A Dialogue of Cultures

The ancestors' rites within the Catholic Church are a manifestation of the degree of acculturation of the Catholic Church in Taiwan, and vice versa, of the degree of acculturation of Taiwanese culture in the Catholic Church. In the previous pages, I pointed out how these types of rituals are the most significant link between the two religions, and more importantly, between the two cultures. By culture, I mean the symbolic system that embodies within itself religious symbols.

Only with this premise, it is possible to analyze and find meaning for the contradictions and contrasts that arise with contact between the two religious systems of the Taiwanese popular religion and the Catholic Church.

Therefore, the main line of inquiry of this work was research based on the acknowledgment of the symbols belonging to both religious cosmologies, and on the understanding of how these symbols establish bridges and bonds between these two cultures. A conspicuous number of works by other anthropologists, particularly those made in Taiwan with the view of analyzing the Taiwanese popular religion, helped me to define the three types of supernatural beings that formulate the Taiwanese popular religion: gods, ancestors, and ghosts. I demonstrated how this type of division is still real for many Catholics in Taiwan, and I analyzed the complex historical encounter between these two different cosmologies and worldviews.

The theoretical background of this research is principally based on the work of two eminent scholars; Marshal Sahlins on the contact between Hawaiian people and Captain Cook[1], and the book written by Tzvetan Todorov about the conquest of America by the Spaniard conquerors led by Cortez[2]. I have chosen these two authors because their works are based on

---

[1]. Sahlins, *Islands of History*.
[2]. Todorov, *The conquest of America*.

7 Conclusions

the cultural analysis of a historical encounter between two different peoples and cultures. From a theoretical point of view, I could not directly relate Sahlins' work with the situation I found in Taiwan, because Sahlins' analysis concerns the contact between a culture and an event, and his analysis deepened at the precise moment of encounter. As I have shown above, the contact between the Catholic Church's cultural world and the Taiwanese cultural contest includes not only the moment of the encounter but a complete historical process. Before arriving in Taiwan, the Catholic Church – and especially the Dominican missionaries – had experienced centuries of evangelization in China, and already passed through the dispute about the Chinese ancestors' rites. During this long time, the events that happened between these two different worldviews molded both the relations between the two cultural systems and the Catholic Church's views about these rites. It is important to remember that the Dominicans, were the only missionaries on the island before 1949, and were fierce adversaries of the Jesuits during the earlier period of China's evangelization. They opposed Ricci's "Indications and Permissions" and prohibited their believers from maintaining their ancestors' tablets and venerating them. This rejection and opposition continue even today, in fact, some of the Dominican Fathers in Taiwan, despite the Church permission, do not allow the use of a "community tablet" in their Churches, because according to them, the missionaries should take account of one of the Han people's tradition: "people outside the family cannot worship my own ancestors". Clearly, if you do not want to allow me to do something, you can easily find many justifications.

What I have borrowed from Sahlins was the idea that this type of relationship should be analyzed within a cultural context. Only by considering and analyzing both cultural systems where these two religions are embodied, is it possible to try to understand their reciprocal relations and how these relations are embodied in the everyday life of the people. Nevertheless, while Sahlin's work analyzes the encounter, the contact, and the cultural explanation of this contact, I felt more attracted to the idea of understanding what happened after the first contact. In other words, I wanted to discover the progression that can be defined as cohabitation and cohabitation between two different cultural systems. Consequentially, I focused my research on what happens to this particular category of people, namely, the Taiwanese Catholics, who embrace and live within two different cultural systems.

Unlike Sahlins and his static structuralist conception of culture, I consider culture as a more dynamic and creative entity. To consider culture as a static structure means losing sight of the many and various situations that are present within the same cultural environment.

7.2 The Place of the Dialogue

If culture is a public system of meanings, everybody who lives in the same cultural context can arbitrarily choose the meaning apt to interpret a specific event. Of course, this arbitrariness is always linked with each individual's existential personality, knowledge, economic situation, etc. Arbitrariness is mediation, a negotiation between the public system of meanings, the particular conditions of everyday life, and the practical circumstances of each person. I want to stress that these two different systems of meaning encounter each other in the space represented by the person. By considering the person as a place of dialogue – dialogue that comprehends all the set of compromises, receptions, etc – the three levels suggested by Todorov (the axiological level with its value judgment, the praxeological one with its action of rapprochement or distancing, and the epistemic one which represents either knowledge or ignorance of the other's identity), are placed in a more dialectical relationship. Inside the space represented by the person, it is possible to evaluate the new symbols, it is possible to accept some of the new symbols and to take a certain distance from others. It is even possible to decide to dislike the new symbols but at the same time be completely ignorant of them. On the other hand, it is possible to choose the New and reject the Old. Moreover, within every person, these options and or choices could be changed rearranged, and realigned in different ways in order to solve old and new problems.

This situation becomes evident in the Taiwanese Catholic context. As seen Catholics in Taiwan live in a completely non-Catholic environment. Oftentimes, only one member of the family is Catholic, while the rest still believes in popular religion. Most of the time, during the Chinese New Year or the Clean Tomb festival, Catholics join their parents in these rituals, praying to their ancestors and sometimes going to the temple to burn incense and offer food to the gods. Several Catholics told me that, during the Lunar New Year celebrations, they go to the Mazu temple just because "my mother asked me so, probably when my mother passes away, I will not go to the temple anymore". As Geertz wrote in "The religion of Java", "religious patterns do not become embodied in social forms directly, purely and simply, but in many devious ways, so that religious commitments and others commitments-to class, neighborhood, etc.- tend to balance off, and various "mixed type" individuals and group arise which can play an important mediating role"[3]. Despite the fact that some points of these two religions seem incompatible, society is built by persons, relationships, neighbors, friends, etc. This fact relaxes the tensions and makes possible a kind of harmony between different beliefs and perspectives of the world. This happens because religious symbols are embodied in a wider symbolic system that we call culture. The symbols chosen by a person do not belong only to the religious

---

3. Clifford Geertz, *The Religion of Java* [in en] (University of Chicago Press, 1976), 356.

7 Conclusions

sphere, because the choice is made from among all the symbols embodied in culture. Thus it can be asserted that in Taiwan, there has been and there still is, contact and a mutual interpretation of the two cultural systems, and within this, dialectical relationship people find the symbols which are apt to give meaning to their everyday life. It is this dialectical encounter that became history: the symbols of one cultural system slowly penetrated and rooted themselves within the other system, and vice versa.

One day during class, our professor shared with us a story about a young woman who arrived with other people from mainland China in Taiwan on a fishing boat. They left Mainland China in order to find a better life, but as soon as they reached Taiwan, the local people killed them. After leaving her body, her soul entered the local temple and started to complain to the god of that community; she complained so much that the god let her enter into another body, a body of an already married woman who died some days before. The professor described this story as a case of resurrection; I was very surprised, so a classmate in order to explain this fact to me said: "Are you not Christian? She resurrected like what happened to your Jesus."

This case aims to explain how the symbols of the new religion have penetrated into Taiwanese culture so that my classmate (a non-Catholic) was able to use a Catholic reference (without perhaps having a full understanding of it) to help me in my understanding of a purely local phenomenon linked to the Taiwanese folk religion. It is evident that there has been a contact, and after the contact, there has been a reciprocal interpretation, an interpretation that not only influenced the Catholics but also, generally speaking, all of the Taiwanese people. It is through these dialectical relationships that people find the symbols apt and able to resolve their problems. Sahlins defined the "structure of conjuncture", as the practical realization of the cultural categories in a specific historical context and as expressed in the interested action of the historical agents, including the microsociology of their interaction[4]. Sahlins stressed the fact that Captain Cook appears as an ancestral god to the Hawaiian priests, but more like a divine warrior to the chiefs; and evidently something else and less to ordinary men and women, and that observing from different perspectives with different social influences objectifying their respective interpretations, people come to a different consensual view. Thus Social communication is as much an empirical gamble as worldly reference[5].

In my view, although I completely agree with Sahlins words, I still believe this concept is not enough to understand the encounter between these two cultures and especially the situation in Taiwan, where these two symbolic systems have already cohabited for a very long time. In today's Taiwanese context, the historical agents are not the Western missionaries, but the Taiwanese people who already live within these two symbolic systems. Everyone who encounters Catholicism, apart from those who convert

---

4. Sahlins, *Islands of History*, xiv.
5. Sahlins, x.

themselves, could be considered an agent of this historical process. Certainly, the agents are Mister Guo or Mister Gao (Chapter 4), the elder brother of Miss Li, and also my classmate who explained to me the concept of Jesus' resurrection. The risks mentioned by Sahlins could only be real when a structure encounters new events, but in the Taiwanese situation, being the person the space where this encounter happens, the two symbolic systems are both present and real, and the change is already present in this place, not only potentially but concretely. As consequence, what Sahlins considers as risks, are not risks but integral parts of the culture; in fact, they *are* culture.

7.3 The Textile of Dialogue

As Geertz has said, the variety of lifestyles arises out of the ways in which the variety of these practices which make them up are positioned and composed. It is not, to adapt Wittgenstein's famous image of a rope, a single thread that runs all the way through them that defines them and makes them into some kind of a whole. It is the overlapping of differing threads, intersecting, entwining, one taking up where another breaks off, all of them posed in effective tensions with one another to form a composite body, "a body locally disparate, globally integral"[6].

In this book, I have attempted to present to the reader this composite body. My point was not to understand how the missionaries (Self) acculturate themselves to the Chinese culture (Other) or how the Chinese worldview (Self) receives or rejects the message of Catholicism (Other) because for me, as an anthropologist, both of them are Others and what I am studying is their dialectical encounter and cohabitation. Adapting this concept to Geertz's metaphor, and borrowing a concept pointed out by Nicolas Standaert[7] it is possible to say that the situation being analyzed is a textile, where what I have described as symbolic systems – and perhaps the symbols itself – are these ropes. Each person arbitrarily – and I still repeat that this arbitrariness is always linked with personality, and existential, practical, situations, etc. – can choose how to weave these ropes. Moreover, as a woven cloth or textile, it is possible both to notice the various colors of the threads and to recognize the shapes these threads form on the textile. Therefore, as Standaert pointed out, between total absorption – the appropriation of a foreign element in its entirety – or total rejection, my textile metaphor reformulates the monochrome cloth with spectrums of infinite combination and permutation. In my view, this metaphor can be used on two different

---

6. Clifford Geertz, "The World in Pieces: Culture and Politics at the End of the Century," in *Available Light: Anthropological Reflections on Philosophical Topics*. (Princeton: Princeton University Press, 1993), 218–263.

7. Standaert, "Contact between Cultures: The Case of Christianity in China (Some Methodological Issues)"; Nicolas Standaert, *The Interweaving of Rituals: Funerals in the Cultural Exchange Between China and Europe* (University of Washington Press, 2008).

levels: the personal and the social levels. On the personal level, the "ropes" are the symbols embodied and embedded within these symbolic systems, while on the social level the "ropes" are the person himself.

According to Standaert, the metaphor of the textile illuminates and illustrates what happens to specific fibers and shows the usage, meaning, form, and function of the textile as a whole. Thus this metaphor helps comprehension of how there can be very different reactions at the same time, within the same person – as Miss Li's parent – or within the same geographical setting – as the Resurrection Parrish – or within the same social group. Therefore, in order to better understand this weave which has been the real object of my research; it was necessary to examine the basis of the two cultural systems.

In addition, at the same time, it is necessary to study the historical weave which made it possible to observe the peculiarity of the present-day weave. In the nowadays historical moment of this encounter, or better, this dialogue is changing more and more. This is brought out in an ambiance (Taipei City) which is involved in the increasing phenomenon of Westernization that is very visible through the architecture, the lifestyles, and the enormous phenomenon of people traveling to the USA or other European countries to study for a Master's Degree or a Ph.D. program, etc. Therefore, the basic context is changing, and the symbolic systems and the symbols and meanings which can be attributed to these symbols are multiplying. On the one hand, the younger generations tend to leave their parent's home early because they study in another city and thus there is no longer any direct experience of ancestors' rites. On the other hand, the influence of the traditional cultural roots remains very strong, and powerful symbolic system in Taiwan. It is true many young people do not have direct experience in performing the rites of their ancestors, but these rites and the family and social responsibilities that they entail are learned when the person must perform them (perhaps because the father is dead). Therefore, existentially, the solution is sought only when the problem arises.

The weave of this textile is becoming more and more complex and multicolored. Only with in-depth knowledge of the "ropes" can there be an appreciation of its diversity of shapes, shades, and colors.

Bibliography

Acta Apostolicae Sedis. *Acta Apostolicae Sedis 1913-12-20: Vol 5 Iss 18* [in English]. Vol. 5. Libreria Editrice Vaticana, 1913. Accessed March 8, 2022. http://archive.org/details/sim_acta-apostolicae-sedis_1913-12-20_5_18.

Addison, James Thayer. "Chinese Ancestor-Worship and Protestant Christianity." *The Journal of Religion* 5, no. 2 (1925): 140–149.

Ahern, Emily M. *The Cult of the Dead in a Chinese Village*. Stanford University Press, 1973.

Ahern, Emily Martin. *Chinese ritual and politics*. Cambridge, etc.: Cambridge University Press, 1981.

Alighieri, Dante. *The De monarchia of Dante Alighieri*. Translated by Aurelia Henry. Cambridge: The Riverside Press, 1904.

Asad, Talal. "Anthropological Conceptions of Religion: Reflections on Geertz." *Man* 18, no. 2 (1983): 237–259.

Batairwa. "What Do You Do When Visiting a Temple." *Quaderni del Centro Studi Asiatico* 1, no. 1 (2006): 70–76.

Batairwa, Paulin Kubuya. *Meaning and Controversy within Chinese Ancestor Religion*. Cham: Springer, 2018.

Bishop, James. *Clifford Geertz – Religion as a "System of Symbols"*, February 2020. Accessed March 9, 2022. https://jamesbishopblog.com/2020/02/08/clifford-geertz-religion-as-a-system-of-symbols/.

Bourdieu, Pierre. *Raisons pratiques: sur la theorie de l'action*. Paris: Editions du Seuil, 1994.

Bresciani, Umberto. "The Future of Christianity in China" [in en]. *Quaderni del Centro Studi Asiatico* 1, no. 3 (2006): 101–111.

Bibliography

Brucker, Joseph. *Matteo Ricci.* The Catholic Encyclopedia. Nihil Obstat, November 1, 1908. Remy Lafort, S.T.D., Censor. Imprimatur. +John Cardinal Farley. New York, 1912. Accessed March 9, 2022. http://www.newadvent.org/cathen/13034a.htm.

Chan, Dy Aristotle S.J. *Weaving a dream: reflections for Chinese-Filipino Catholics today.* Quezon City: Jesuit Communications, 2000.

Chen Jia-lu 陳嘉陸. *Tianzhujiao yibainian jianshi* 天主教一百年簡史. Kaohsiung: Youying Press, 1960.

Chen, I-Chun 陳怡君. "宗教經驗的召喚與祖先記憶的重塑：屏東萬金天主教徒的記憶、儀式與認同" [in zh]. PhD Thesis, 國立臺灣大學, January 2011.

Chomsky, Noam. *Cartesian linguistics: a chapter in the history of rationalist thought.* New York: Harper & Row, 1966.

———. *Syntactic structures* [in English]. The Hague: Mouton, 1957.

———. *Topics in the theory of generative grammar.* The Hague: Mouton, 1966.

Clart, Philip. "Popular Religion" as an Analytical Category in the Study of Chinese 158 Religions." In *The Fourth Fu Jen University International Sinological Symposium. Research on Religions in China: Status quo and Perspective.* Edited by Zbigniew Wesolowski, SVD, 166–203. Taipei: Fujen University Press, 2006.

Conference, Taiwan Bishops. 主日感恩祭典(甲). Taipei: 天主教教務協進會出版社, 1983.

Doumont, Louis. "A Modified View of our Origins: the Christian Beginnings of Modern Individualism." In *The Category of the Person: Anthropology, Philosophy, History*, Michael Carrithers, Steven Collins, Steven Lukes, eds, 93–122. Cambridge: Cambridge University Press., 1985.

Durkheim, Emile. *Les formes élémentaires de la vie religieuse. Le système totémique en Australie* [in Français]. 1968, cinquième édition. Paris: Les Presses Universitaires de France, 1912. Accessed March 8, 2022. http://classiques.uqac.ca/classiques/Durkheim_emile/formes_vie_religieuse/formes_vie_religieuse.html.

Feuchtwang, Stephan. "Domestic and communal worship in Taiwan." In *Religion and ritual in Chinese society*, 105–129. Arthur P. Wolf (Editor). Stanford University Press., 1974.

———. *Popular religion in China: the imperial metaphor.* Richmond: Curzon, 2001.

Freedman, Maurice. *Lineage organization in Southeastern China*. Monographs on social anthropology / London School of Economics, no. 18. London: Athlone Press, 1958.

———. *The Study of Chinese Society. Essays Selected and Introduced by G. William Skinner*. Stanford: Stanford University Press, 1979. Accessed March 8, 2022.

GCatholic.org. *Catholic Church in Taiwan*, 2022. Accessed March 9, 2022. http://www.gcatholic.org/dioceses/country/TW.htm.

Geertz, Clifford. *Interpretation of Cultures: Selected Essays*. New York: Basic Books, 1973.

———. "Religion as a Cultural System." In *The interpretation of cultures: selected essays*, 87–125. New York: Basic Books, 1973.

———. *The Religion of Java* [in en]. University of Chicago Press, 1976.

———. "The World in Pieces: Culture and Politics at the End of the Century." In *Available Light: Anthropological Reflections on Philosophical Topics*. 218–263. Princeton: Princeton University Press, 1993.

———. "Time, Person and Conduct in Bali." In *The interpretation of cultures: selected essays*, 360–411. New York: Basic Books, 1973.

Government Information Office Republic of China. *Taiwan Yearbook 2006*. 1st edition. Taipei: the Government Information Office, 2006.

Gramsci, Antonio, Valentino Gerratana, and Istituto Gramsci. *Quaderni del carcere*. Torino: G. Einaudi, 1975.

Harrell, Stevan. "The ancestors at home: domestic worship in a land-poor Taiwanese village." In *Ancestors*, 373–385. Edited by William H. Newell. The Hague, 1976.

Hodgen, Margaret T. *Early anthropology in the sixteenth and seventeenth centuries*. Philadelphia: University of Pennsylvania Press, 1964.

Hsu, Francis. *Under the Ancestors' Shadow: Kinship, Personality, and Social Mobility in Village China*. Stanford University Press, 1967.

Hu, Anning. "Ancestor Worship in Contemporary China: An Empirical Investigation." Publisher: The Chinese University of Hong Kong Press, *China Review* 16, no. 1 (2016): 169–186.

Hulme, Peter. "The Spontaneous Hand of Nature: Savagery, Colonialism, and the Enlightenment." In *The Enlightenment and its shadows*, edited by L. J. Jordanova, 16–34. London ; New York: Routledge, 1990.

Jochim, Christian. "Flowers, Fruit, and Incense Only: Elite versus Popular in Taiwan's Religion of the Yellow Emperor." *Modern China* 16, no. 1 (January 1990): 3–38.

Johnson, Dale A. *Searching for Jesus on the silk road*. [in English]. Lulu Com, 2013.

Jordan, David K. *Gods, ghosts, and ancestors: the folk religion of a Taiwanese village*. Berkeley: University of California Press, 1972.

Lazzarotti, Marco. *Place, Alterity and Narration in a Taiwanese Catholic Village*. Asian Christianity in the Diaspora. Cham: Palgrave Macmillan, 2020.

Legge, James. *Confucian analects: The great learning, and the doctrine of the mean*. New York: Dover Publications, 1971.

———. *The works of Mencius* [in Chinese and English]. New York: Dover Publications, 1970.

Leung, Beatrice K. F. "The Introduction." In *The Catholic Church in Taiwan: Birth, Growth and Development*, edited by Francis K.H. So, Beatrice K.F. Leung, and Ellen Mary Mylod, 1–14. Christianity in Modern China. Singapore: Springer, 2018.

Li, Dan J. *China in Transition: 1517–1911*. New York: Van Nostrand Reinhold Company, 1969.

Li, Yih-yuan. "Chinese geomancy and ancestor worship: a further discussion." In *Ancestors*, 329–338. Edited by William H. Newell. De Gruyter Mouton, 1976.

Lozada, Eriberto P. *God Aboveground: Catholic Church, Postsocialist State, and Transnational Processes in a Chinese Village*. Stanford University Press, 2001.

Lumen gentium. *Lumen gentium*, 1964. Accessed March 8, 2022. https://www.vatican.va/archive/hist_councils/ii_vatican_council/documents/vat-ii_const_19641121_lumen-gentium_en.html.

Luttio, Mark D. "The Chinese Rites Controversy (1603-1742): a Diachronic and Synchronic Approach." *Worship* 68 (1994): 290–313.

Madsen, Richard. "Catholicism as Chinese Folk Religion." In *China and Christianity: Burdened Past, Hopeful Future: Burdened Past, Hopeful Future*, edited by Stephen Uhalley and Xiaoxin Wu. New York: Routledge, 2001.

———. *China's Catholics: Tragedy and Hope in an Emerging Civil Society* [in en]. University of California Press, 1998. ISBN: 9780520213265.

Meldrum, W. *A Cardinal Comes of Age* [in en]. website, September 2005. Accessed March 9, 2022. https://taiwantoday.tw/news.php?unit=20&post=24892.

Menegon, Eugenio. "Yongzheng's Conundrum. The Emperor on Christianity, Religions, and Heterodoxy." In *Rooted in Hope: China – Religion – Christianity*, edited by Barbara Hoster, Dirk Kuhlmann, and Wesolowski Zbigniew, 311–335. Sankt Augustin: Institut Monumenta Serica, 2017.

Minamiki, George. *The Chinese rites controversy from its beginning to modern times*. Chicago: Loyola University Press, 1985.

Missal, Roman. "Eucharistic Prayers I–IV." In *Roman Missal*, Third Typical Edition. Vatican City: Congregation for Divine Worship / the Discipline of the Sacraments, 2001.

Morris Wu, Eleanor B. *From China to Taiwan. Historical, Anthropological, and Religious Perspectives*. Monumenta Serica Institute, 2004.

Motte, Joseph S.J. 天主教史. Taizhong: Guanqi 光文化事業, 1964.

Obeyesekere, Gananath. *The Apotheosis of Captain Cook*. Princeton: Princeton University Press, 1992.

Sahlins, Marshall. *How "Natives" Think: About Captain Cook, For Example*. University of Chicago Press, October 1996.

———. *Islands of History*. University of Chicago Press, 1985.

Sangren, P. Steven. *History and Magical Power in a Chinese Community*. Stanford: Stanford University Press, 1987.

Second Vatican Council Fathers. "Sacrosanctum concilium." In *Documents of the II Vatican Council*. Vatican City: LEV, 1963.

Simmel, Georg. "The Stranger." Translated by Ramona Mosse. *The Baffler* 30, no. 30 (2016): 176–179.

Standaert, Nicolas. "Contact between Cultures: The Case of Christianity in China (Some Methodological Issues)." In 輔仁大學第四屆漢學國際研討會「中國宗教研究：現況與展望」論文集, edited by Wesolowski Zbigniew. Taipei: Fujen University Press, 2002.

———. "Matteo Ricci: Shaped by the Chinese." *China Heritage Quarterly* 23 (2010): 1–8.

———. *The Interweaving of Rituals: Funerals in the Cultural Exchange Between China and Europe*. University of Washington Press, 2008.

Standaert, Nicolas S.J. "New Trends in the Historiography of Christianity in China." *The Catholic Historical Review* 83, no. 4 (1997): 573–613.

Bibliography

Teiser, Stephen F. *The Ghost Festival in Medieval China*. Princeton University Press, 1988.

Todorov, Tzvetan. *The conquest of America: the question of the other*. Norman: University of Oklahoma Press, 1999.

Todorov, Tzvetan, and Wlad Godzich. *Mikhail Bakhtin: the dialogical principle*. Minneapolis: University of Minnesota Press, 1984.

Treaties of Tianjin. *1858, Tianjin – France / china's external relations – a history*, March 2016. Accessed March 9, 2022. https://web.archive.org/web/20160305022918/http://www.chinaforeignrelations.net/node/162.

Turner, Victor. *The Ritual Process: Structure and Anti-Structure*. Transaction Publishers, 1995.

Verbiest, Study Note. *Special Issue on the Catholic Church in Taiwan: 1626–1965*. Vol. 16. Taipei: Published occasionally by the China Program of the CICM SM Province, 2004.

Verhelst, D., and Nestor Pycke. *C.I.C.M. Missionaries, Past and Present, 1862-1987: History of the Congregation of the Immaculate Heart of Mary (Scheut/Missionhurst)*. Leuven University Press, 1995.

Wang, Sung-hsing. "Ancestors proper and peripheral." In *Ancestors*, 365–372. Edited by William H. Newell. De Gruyter Mouton, 1976.

———. "Taiwanese architecture and the supernatural." In *Religion and ritual in Chinese society*. Stanford: Stanford University Press, 1974.

Watson, James L. "The Structure of Chinese Funerary Rites: Elementary Forms, Ritual Sequence, and the Primacy of Performance." In *Death ritual in late imperial and modern China*, edited by James L. Watson, Evelyn Sakakida Rawski, and Joint Committee on Chinese Studies (U.S.), 3–19. Berkeley: University of California Press, 1988.

Weller, Robert. *Resistance, Chaos and Control in China: Taiping Rebels, Taiwanese Ghosts and Tiananmen*. University of Washington Press, 1994.

———. *Unities and Diversities in Chinese Religion*. University of Washington Press, 1983.

Wolf, Arthur P. "Aspects of ancestor worship in northern Taiwan." In *Ancestors*, 339–364. The Hague; Paris: Mouton Publishers, 1976.

———. "Chinese Kinship and Mourning Dress." In *Family and kinship in Chinese society*. Edited by Ai-li S Chin, Maurice Freedman, Joint Committee on Contemporary China, and Subcommittee on Research on Chinese Society, 189–207. Stanford, Calif.: Stanford University Press, 1970.

———. "Gods, ghosts, and ancestors." In *Religion and ritual in Chinese society*, 131–182. Stanford: California : Univ. Pr, 1974.

Yu, Chun-Fang. *Kuan-yin: The Chinese Transformation of Avalokiteśvara*. Columbia University Press, 2001.

Yu Ying-Shih 余英時. "中國古代死後世界觀的演變." In 中國思想傳統的現代詮釋, II. Taipei: 聯經出版事業公司, 1987.

Zhou, Yonglan 周用蘭. "從社會人類學的觀點看臺灣一個新興宗教：軒轅教.", National Taiwan University, 1972.

Zurcher, Erik. *The Buddhist conquest of China: the spread of adaptation of Buddhism in Early Medieval China*. OCLC: 488646391. Leiden: Brill, 2007.

中國主教團禮儀委員會Bishop Conference of China. 殯葬禮儀. Taipei: Xiuding, 1989.

林瑋嬪Wei-ping Lin. "「鬼母找女婿」：鬼、三片壁、與貪婪的研究." 考古人類學刊 1, no. 75 (2011): 13–36.

Printing and Binding
Books on Demand GmbH
In de Tarpen 42, 22848 Norderstedt, Germany